THE
LILAC FAIRY BOOK

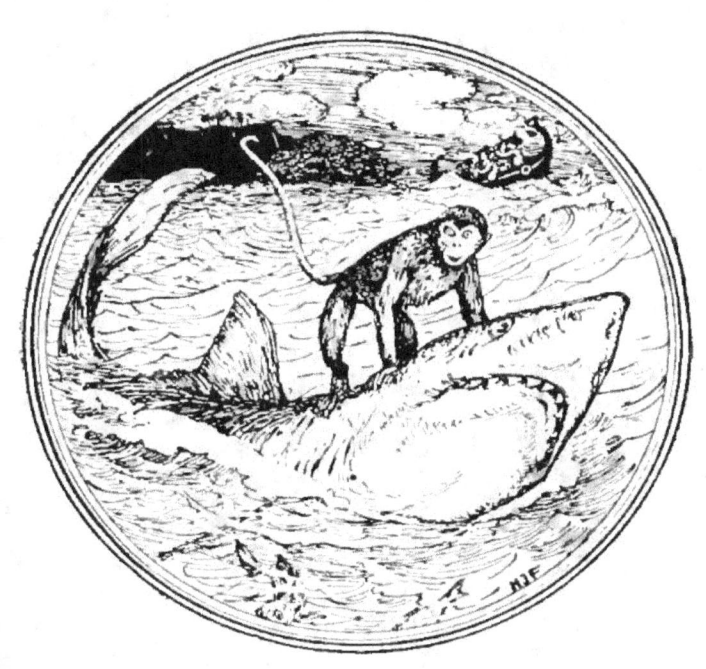

WITH
NUMEROUS ILLUSTRATIONS BY H. J. FORD

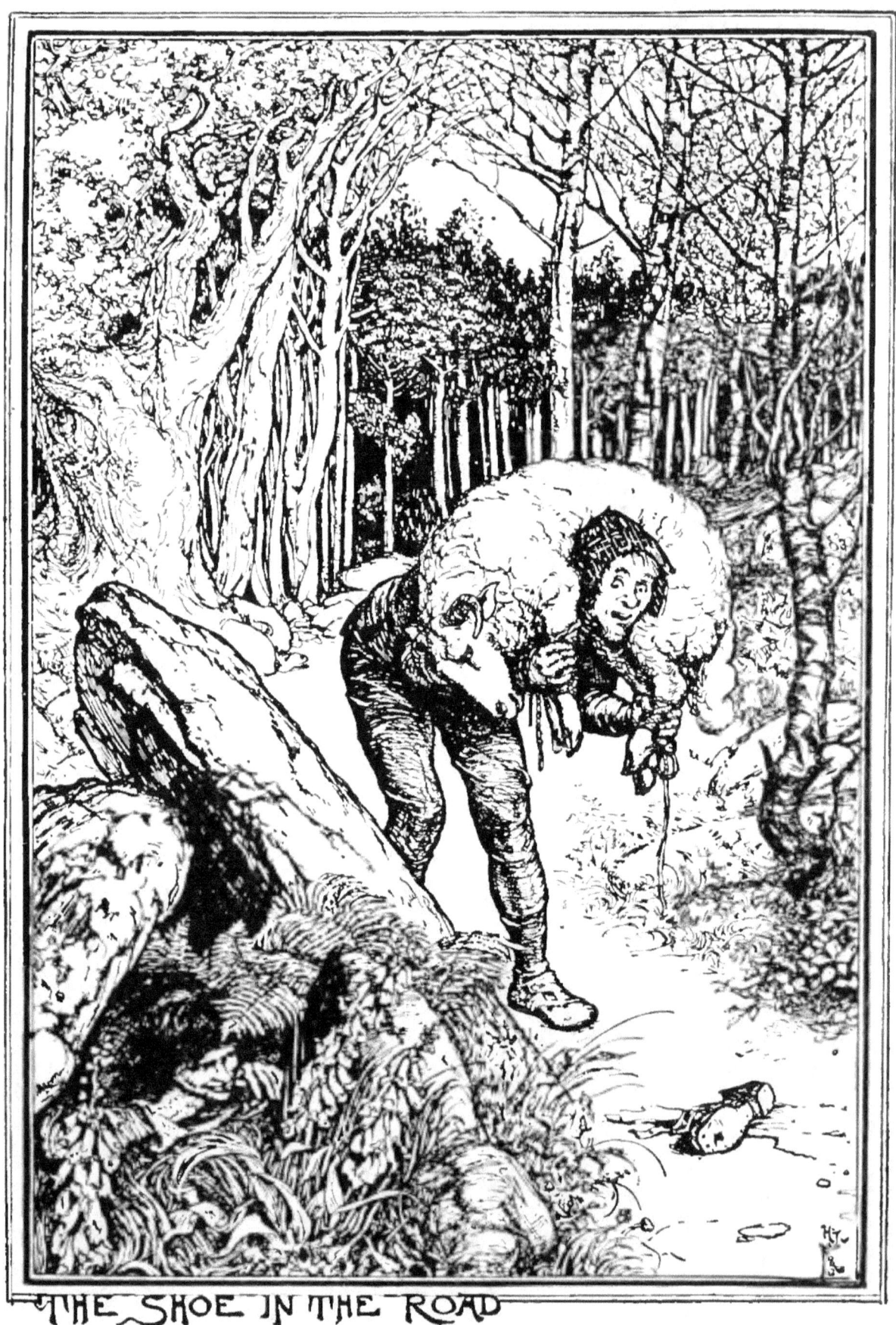

THE SHOE IN THE ROAD

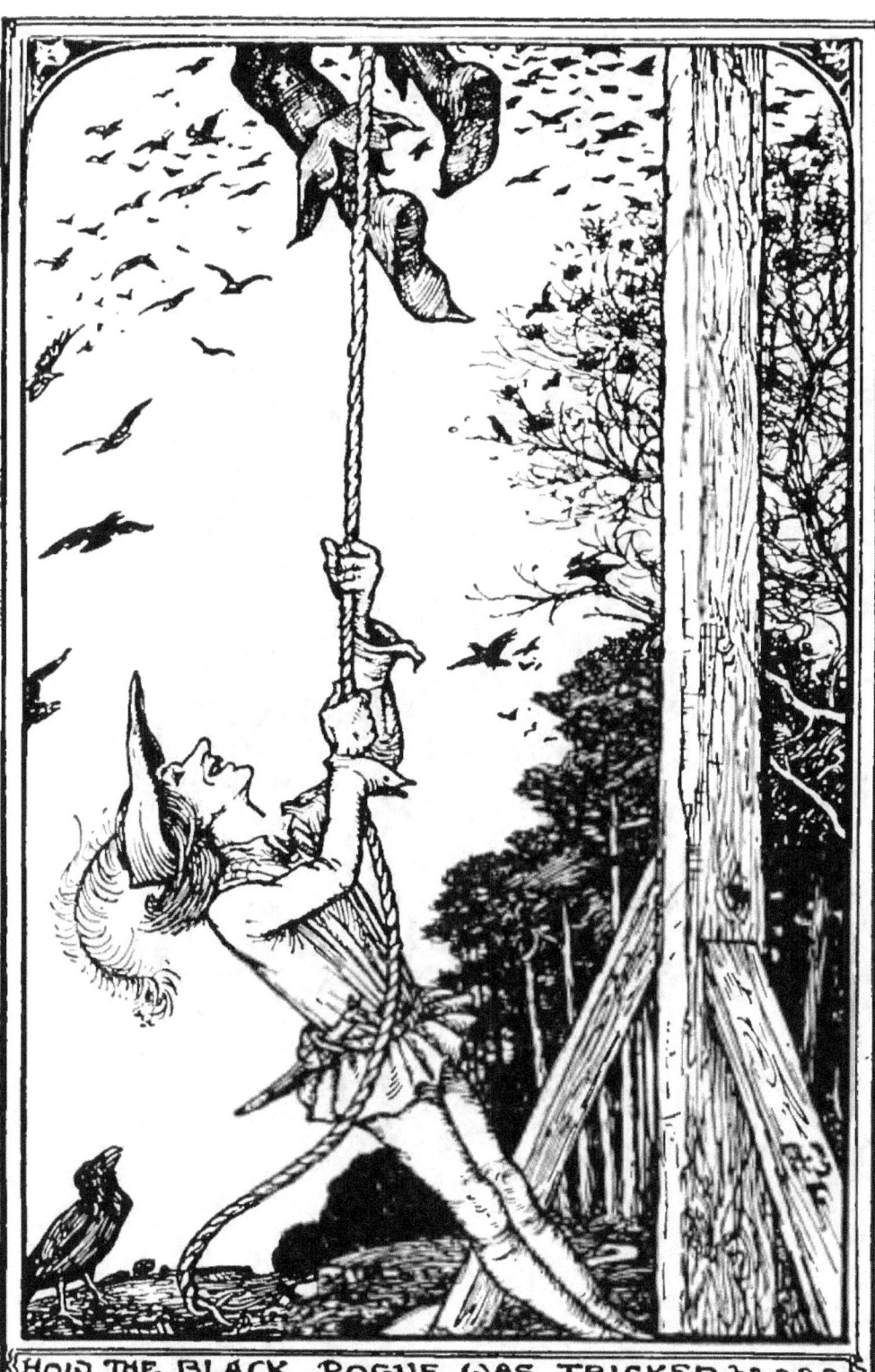
HOW THE BLACK ROGUE WAS TRICKED

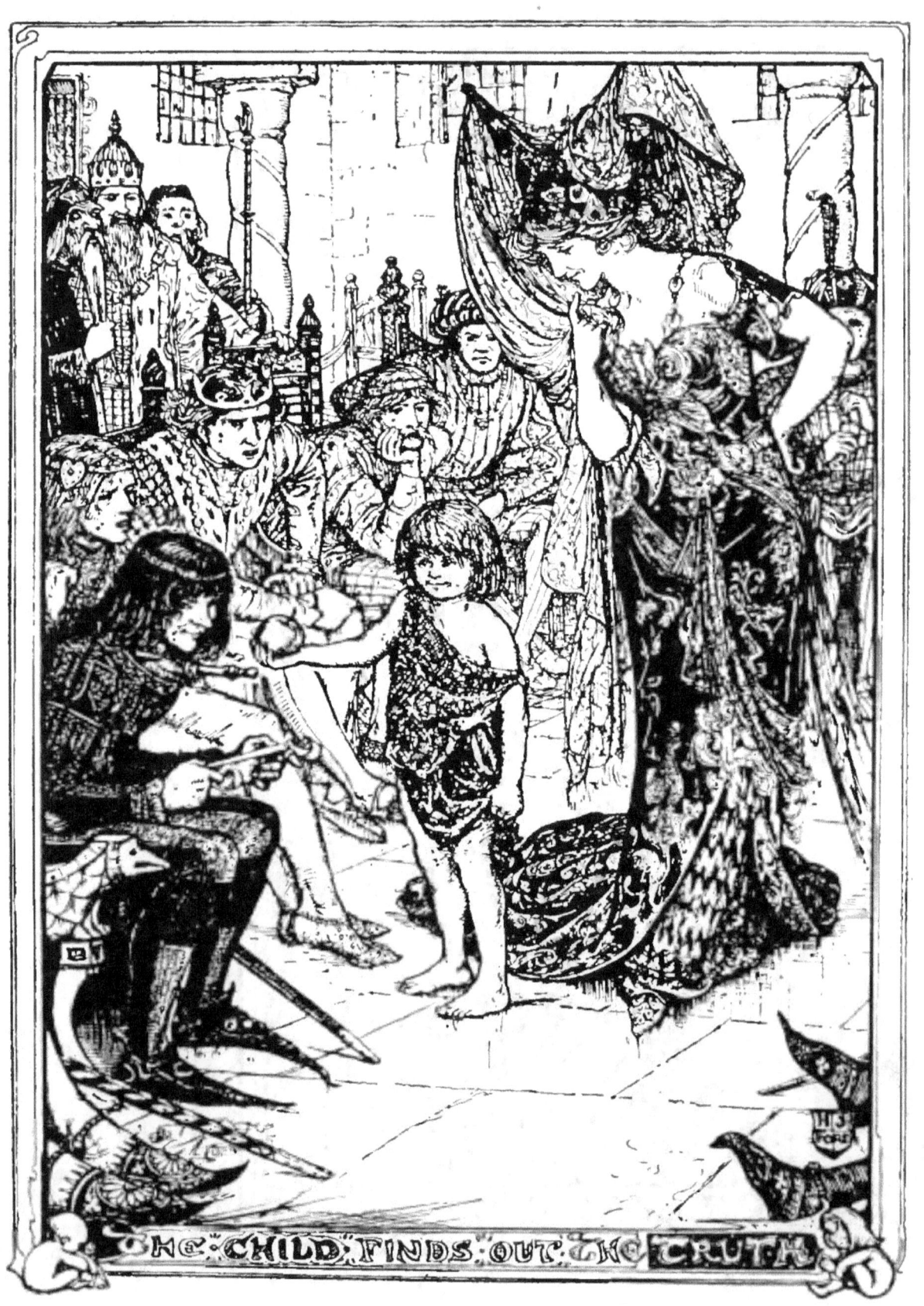
THE CHILD FINDS OUT THE TRUTH

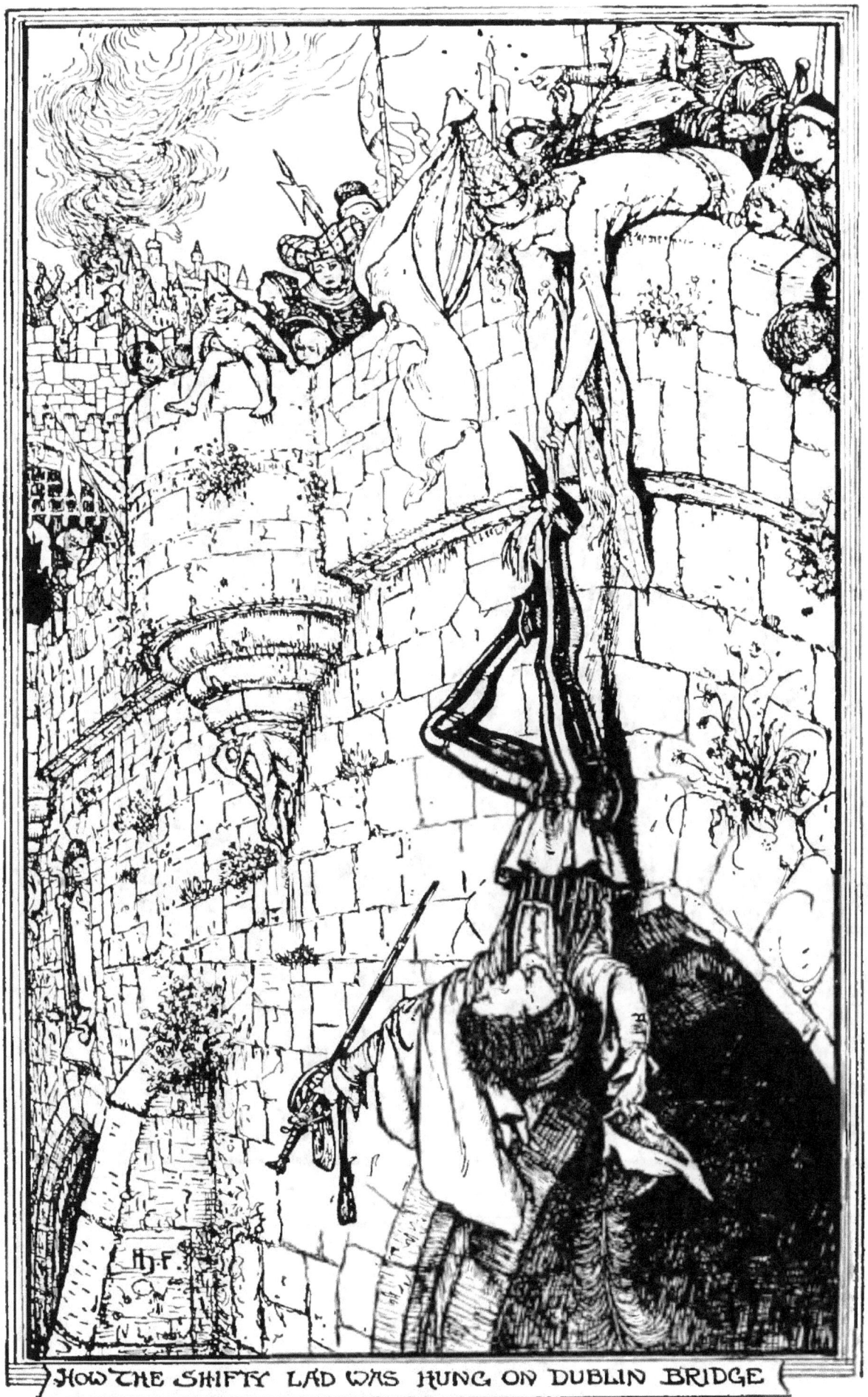

HOW THE SHIFTY LAD WAS HUNG ON DUBLIN BRIDGE

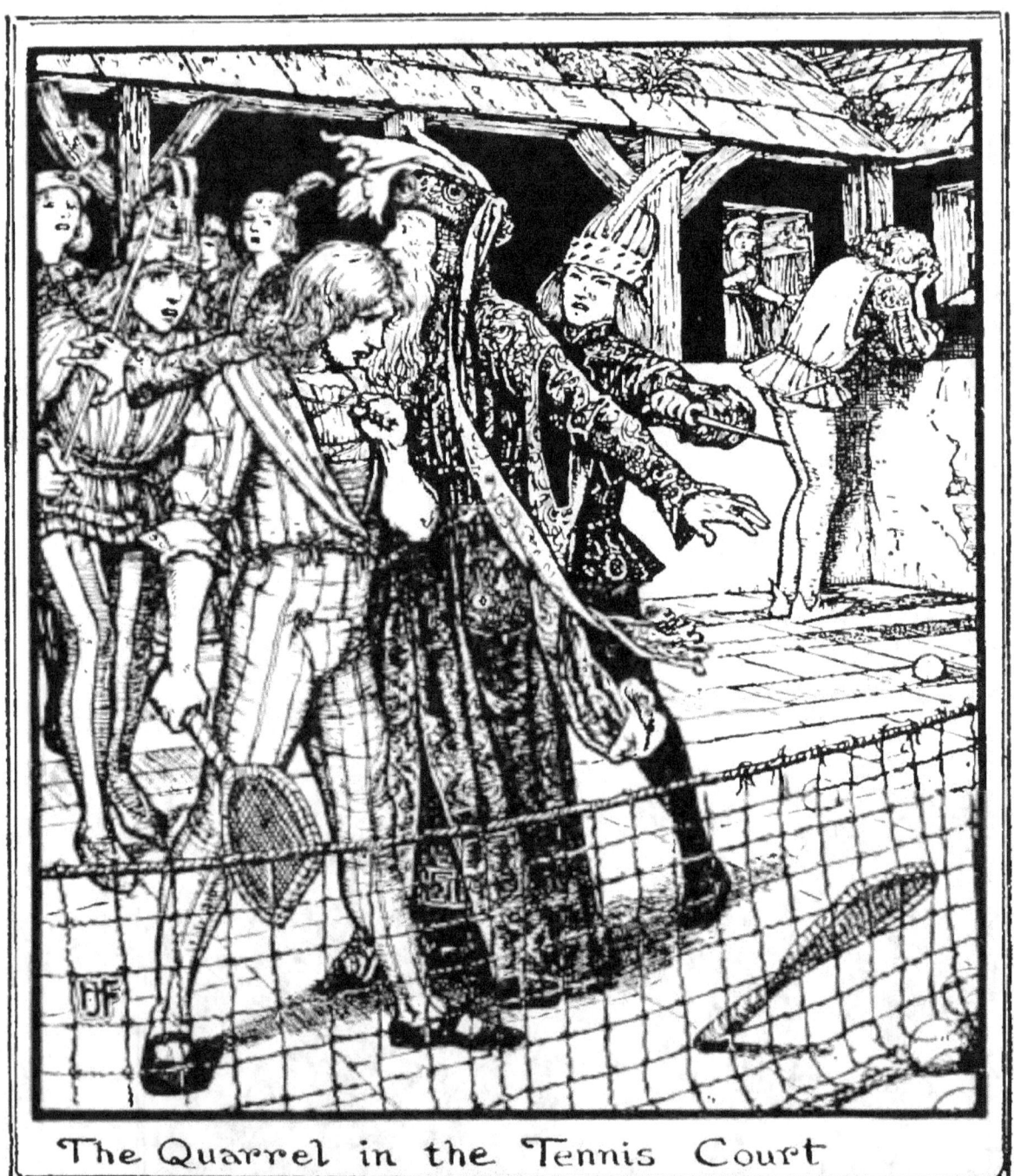

The Quarrel in the Tennis Court

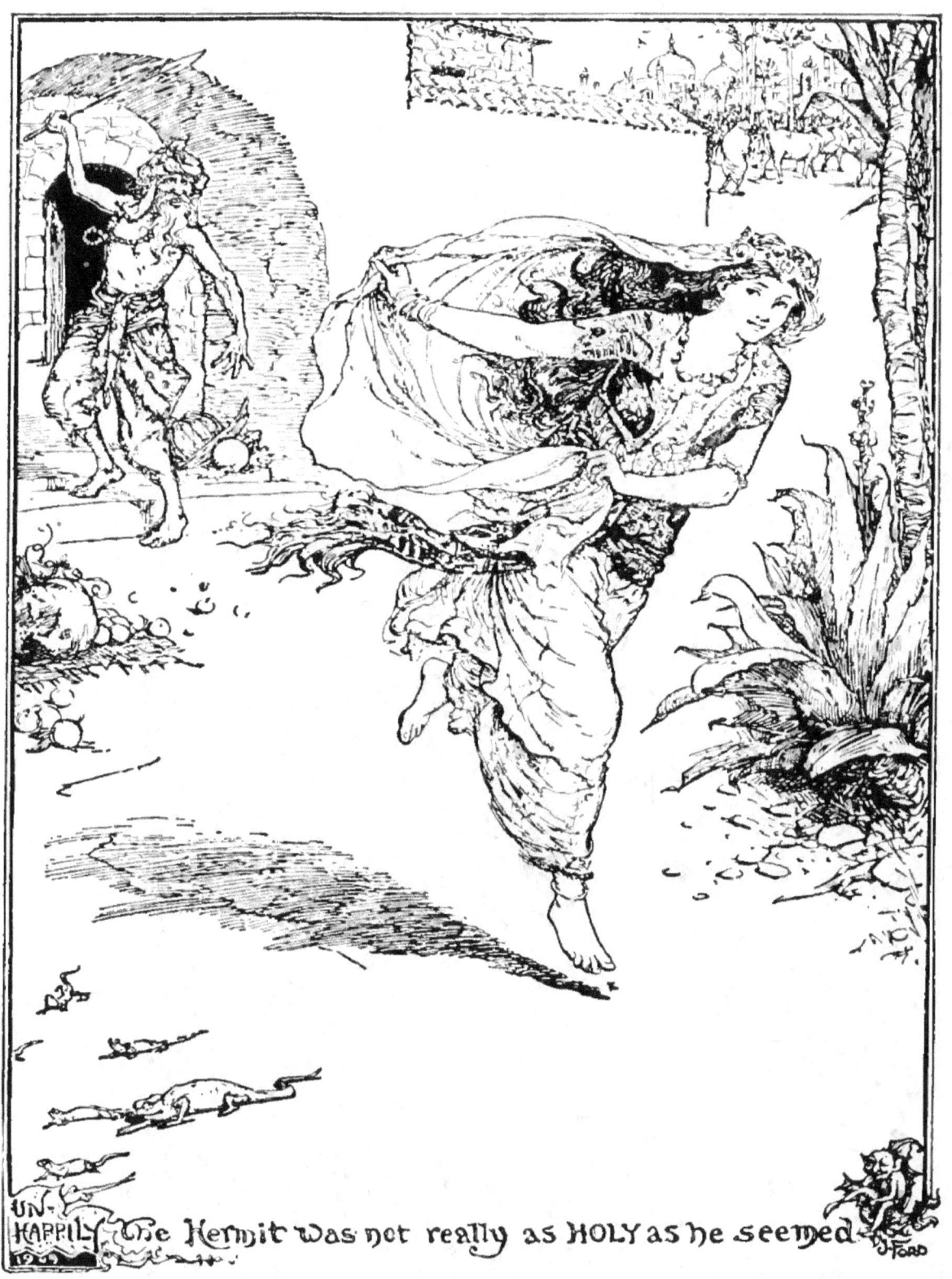
UN-HAPPILY the Hermit was not really as HOLY as he seemed

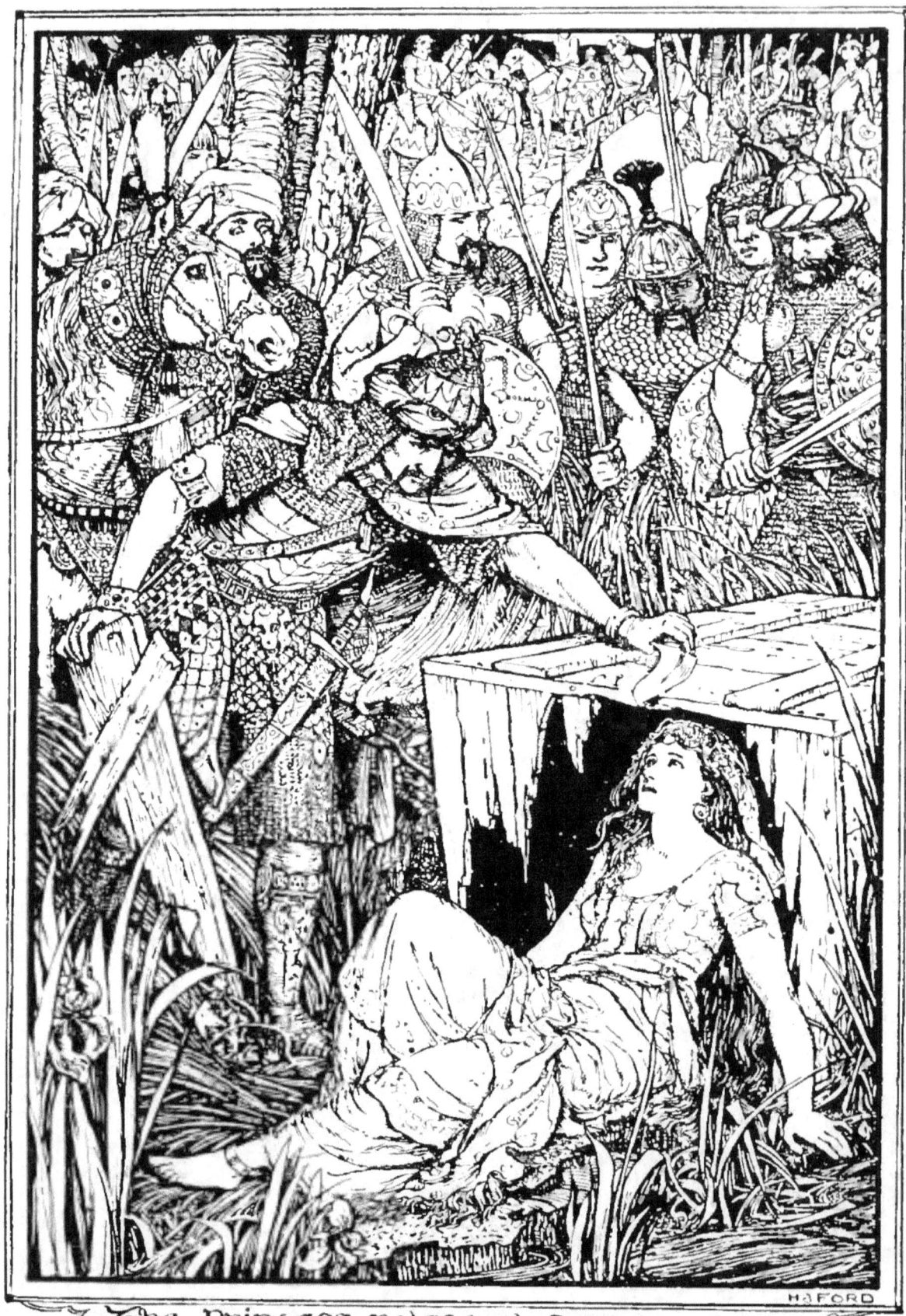
The Princess released from the box

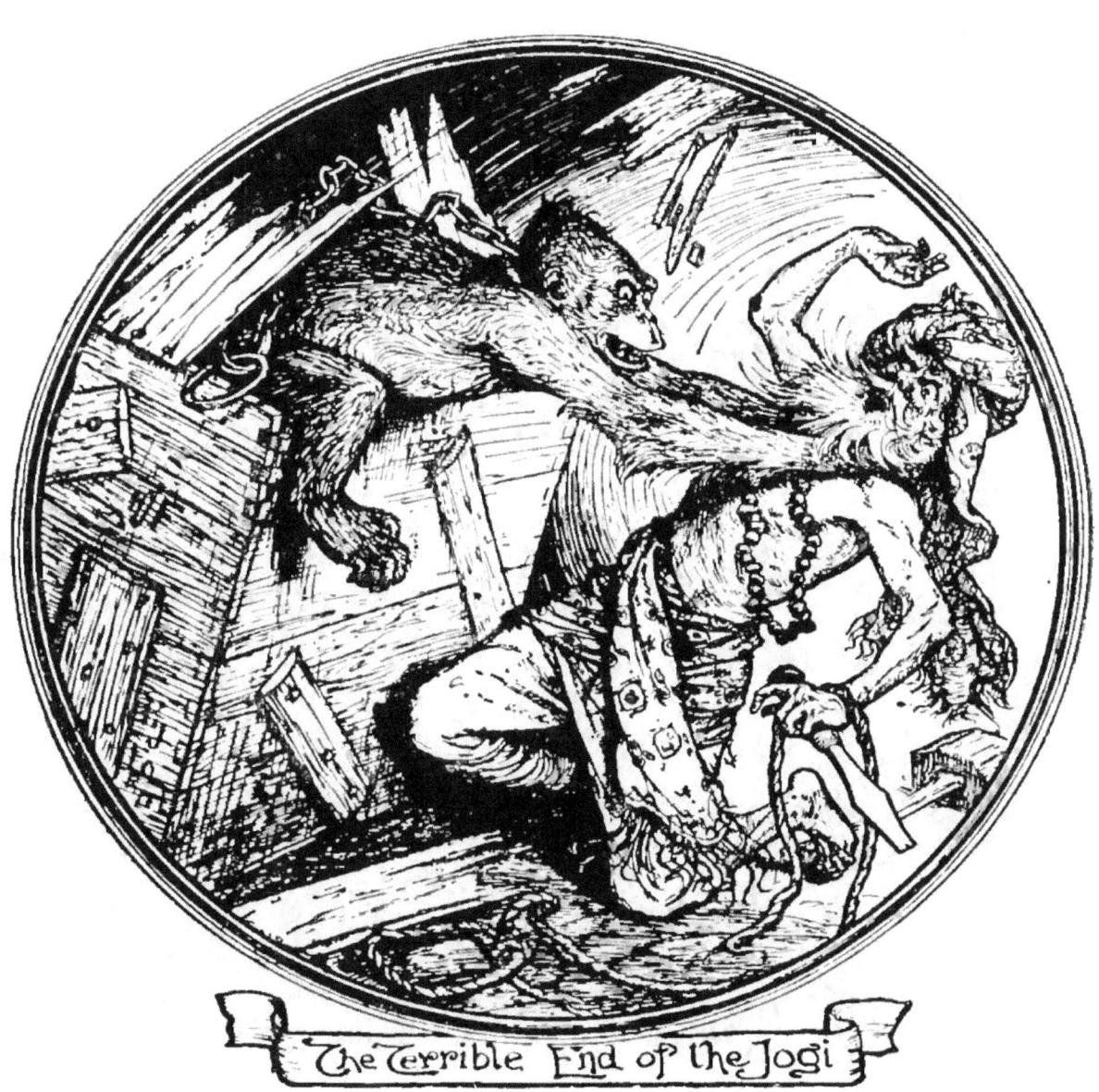
The Terrible End of the Jogi

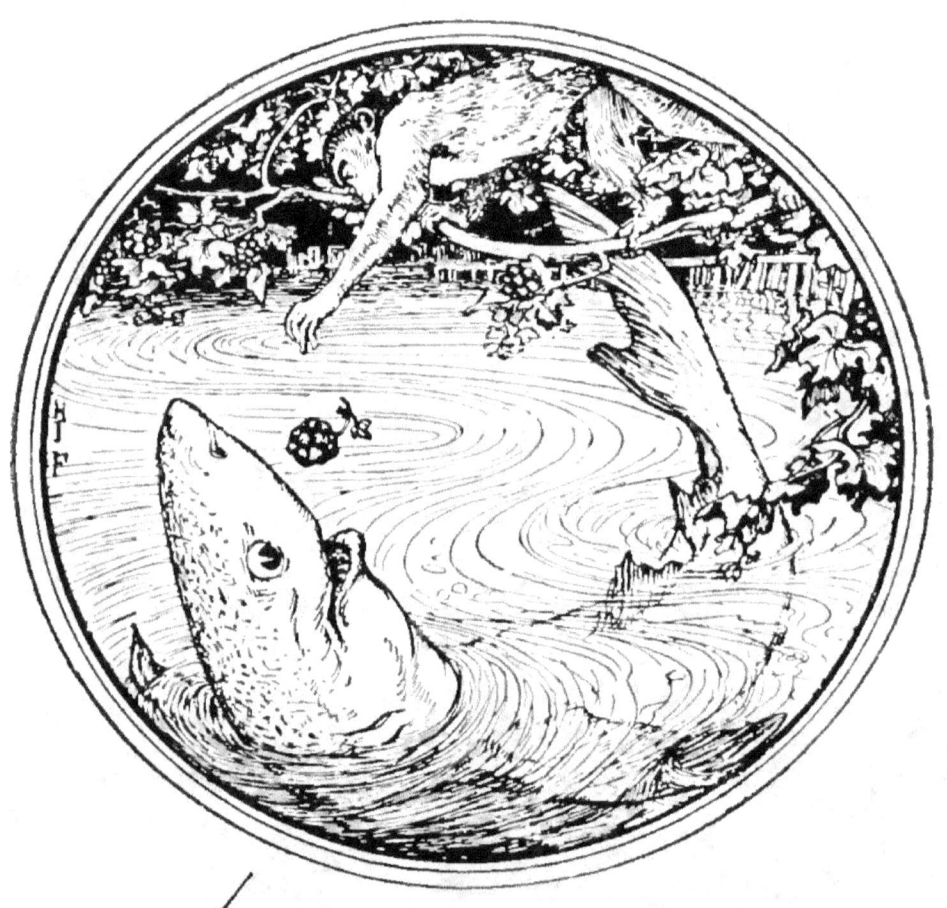

The Monkey feeds the Shark

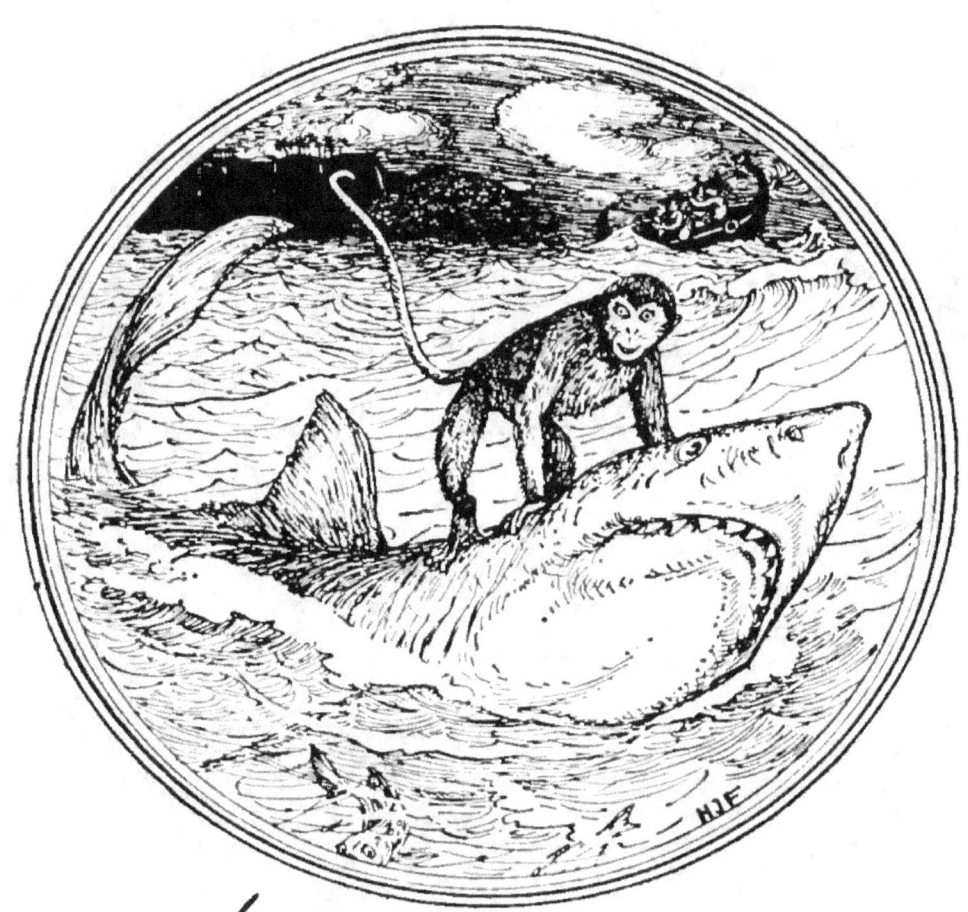

The Monkey has a ride

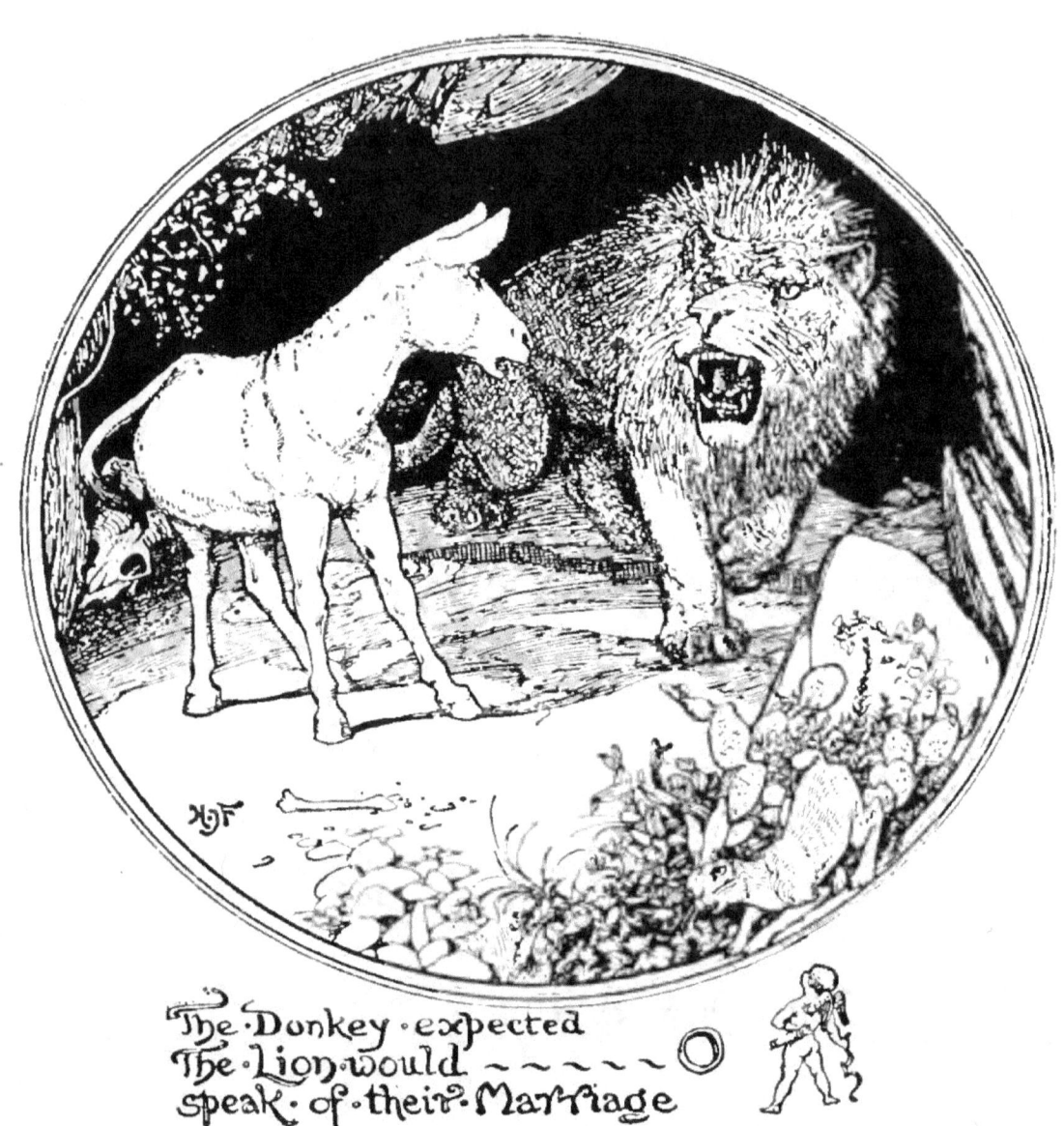

The Donkey expected
The Lion would ~~~~~
speak of their Marriage

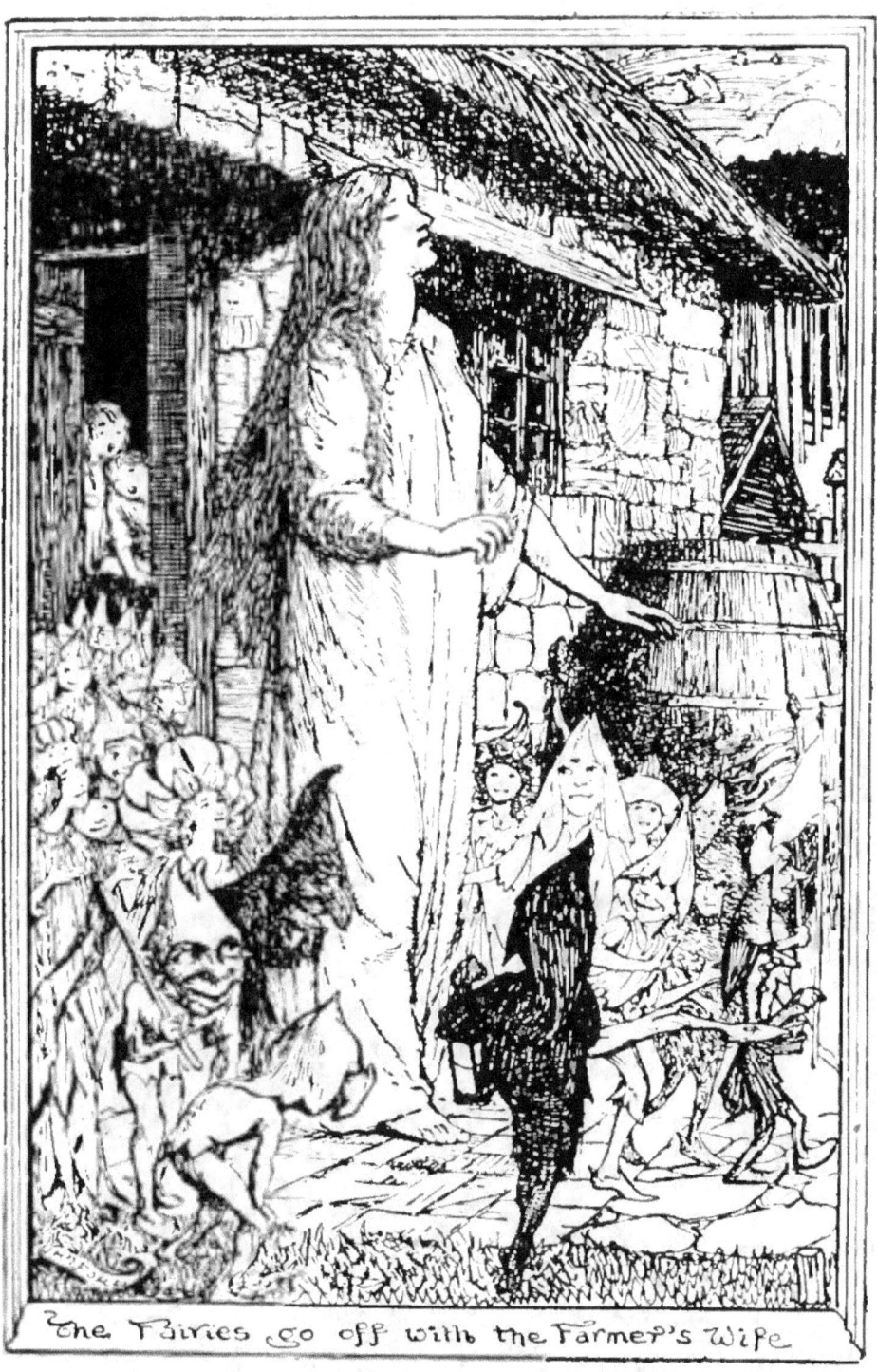

The Fairies go off with the Farmer's Wife

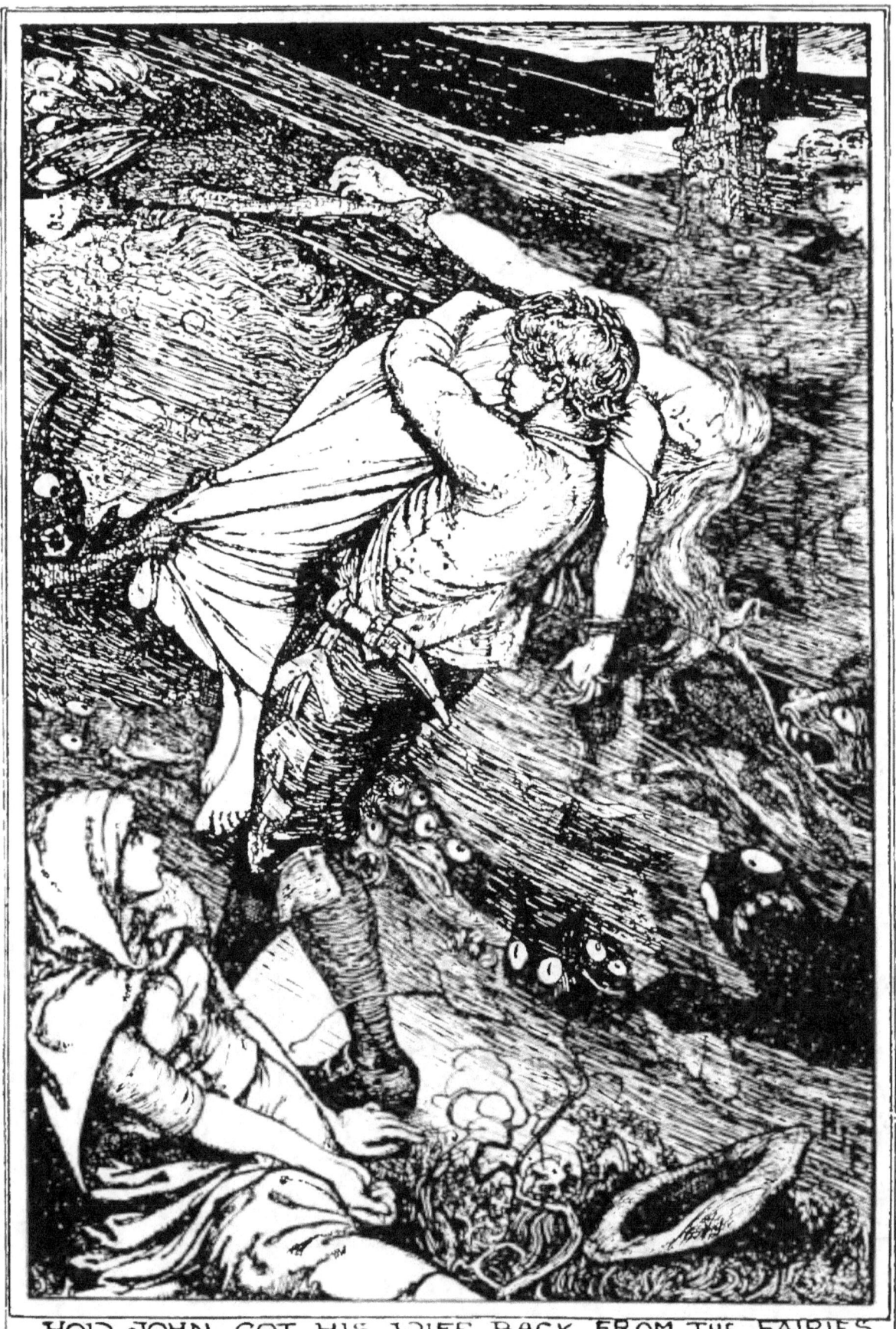
HOW JOHN GOT HIS WIFE BACK FROM THE FAIRIES

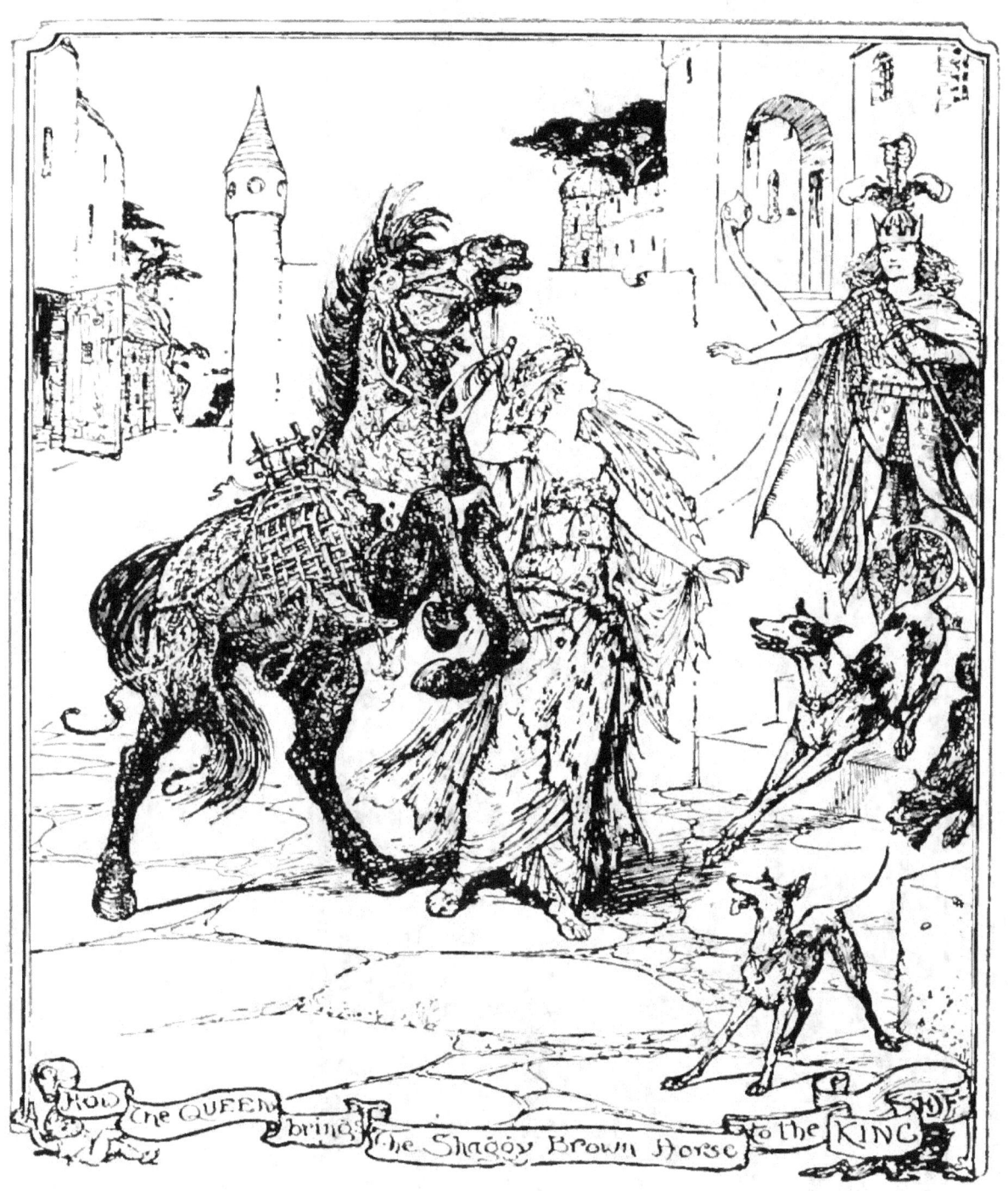

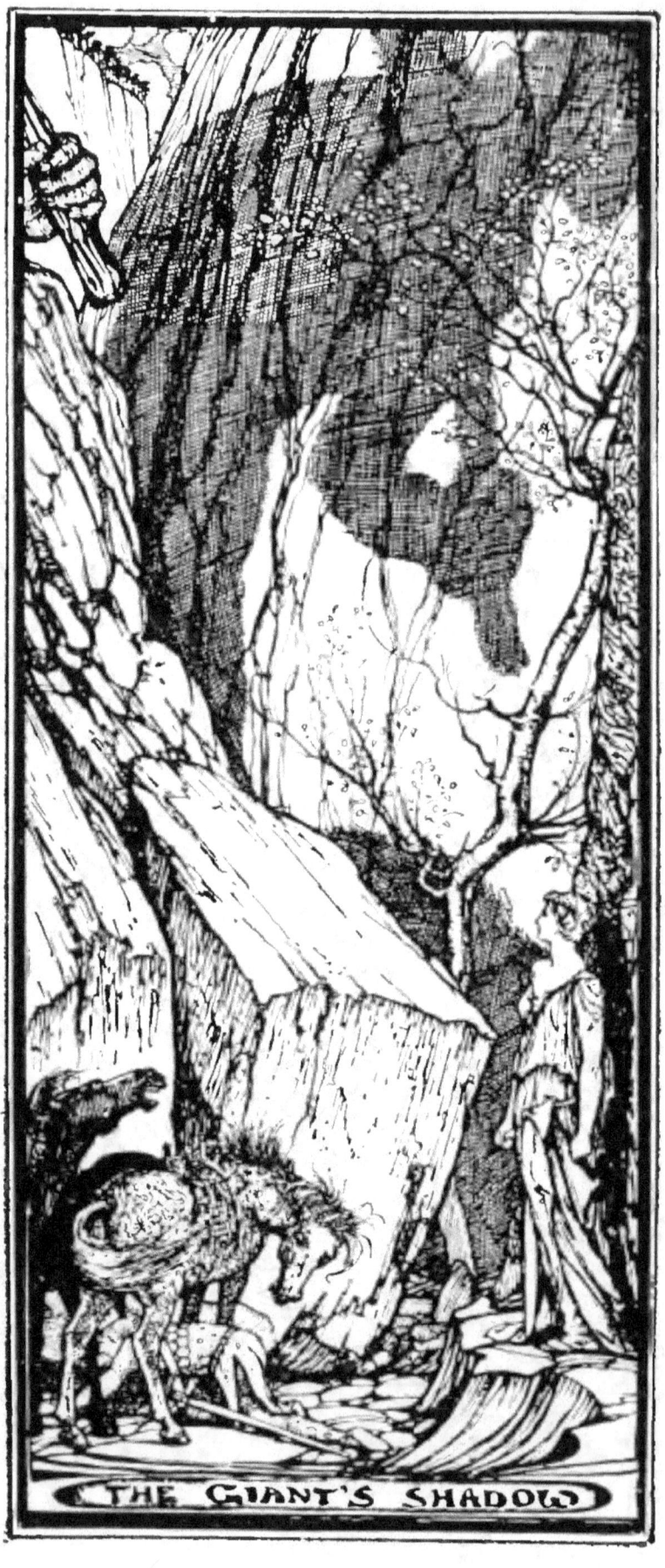
THE GIANT'S SHADOW

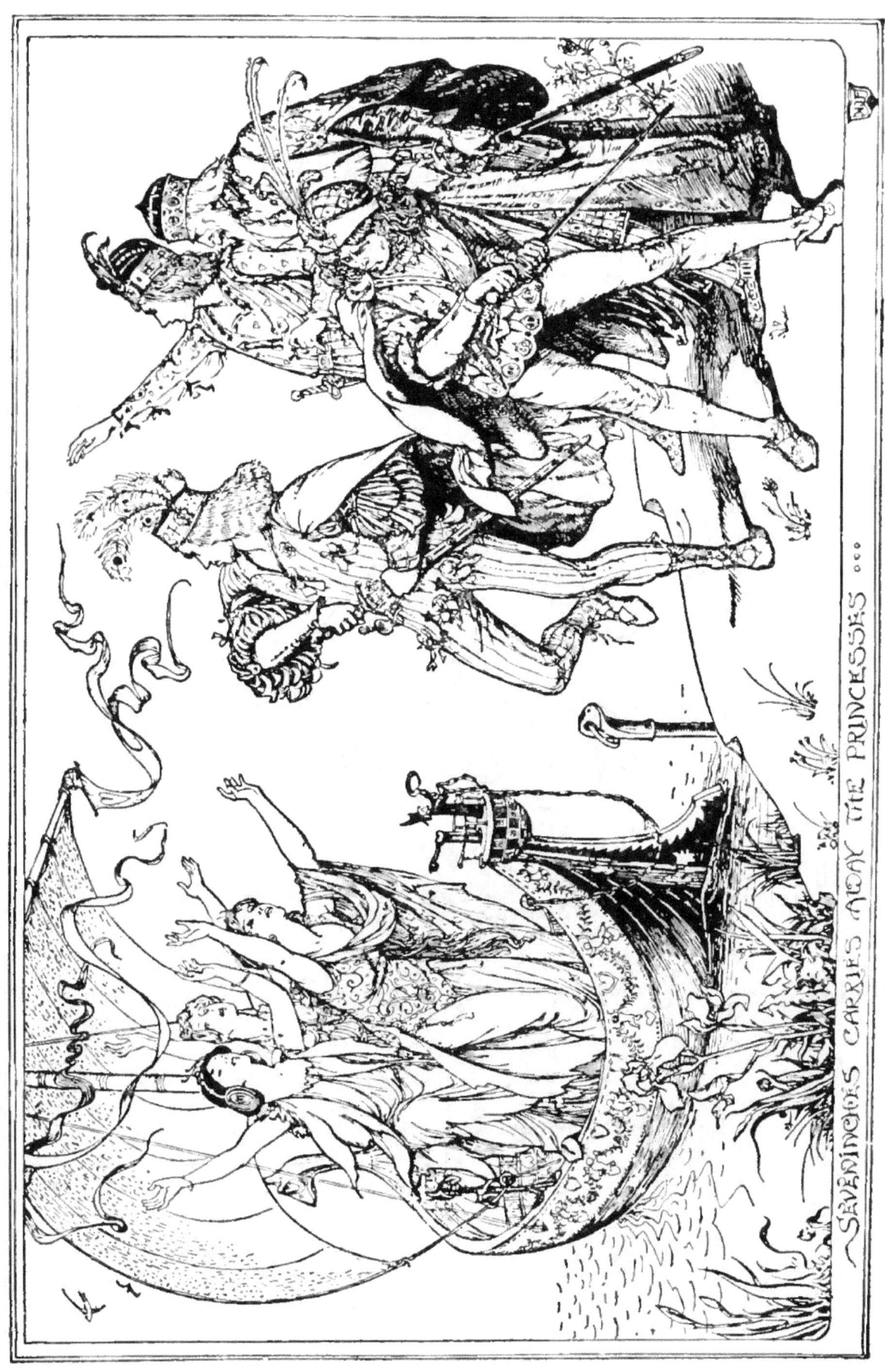
... SEVENWITS CARRIES AWAY THE PRINCESSES ...

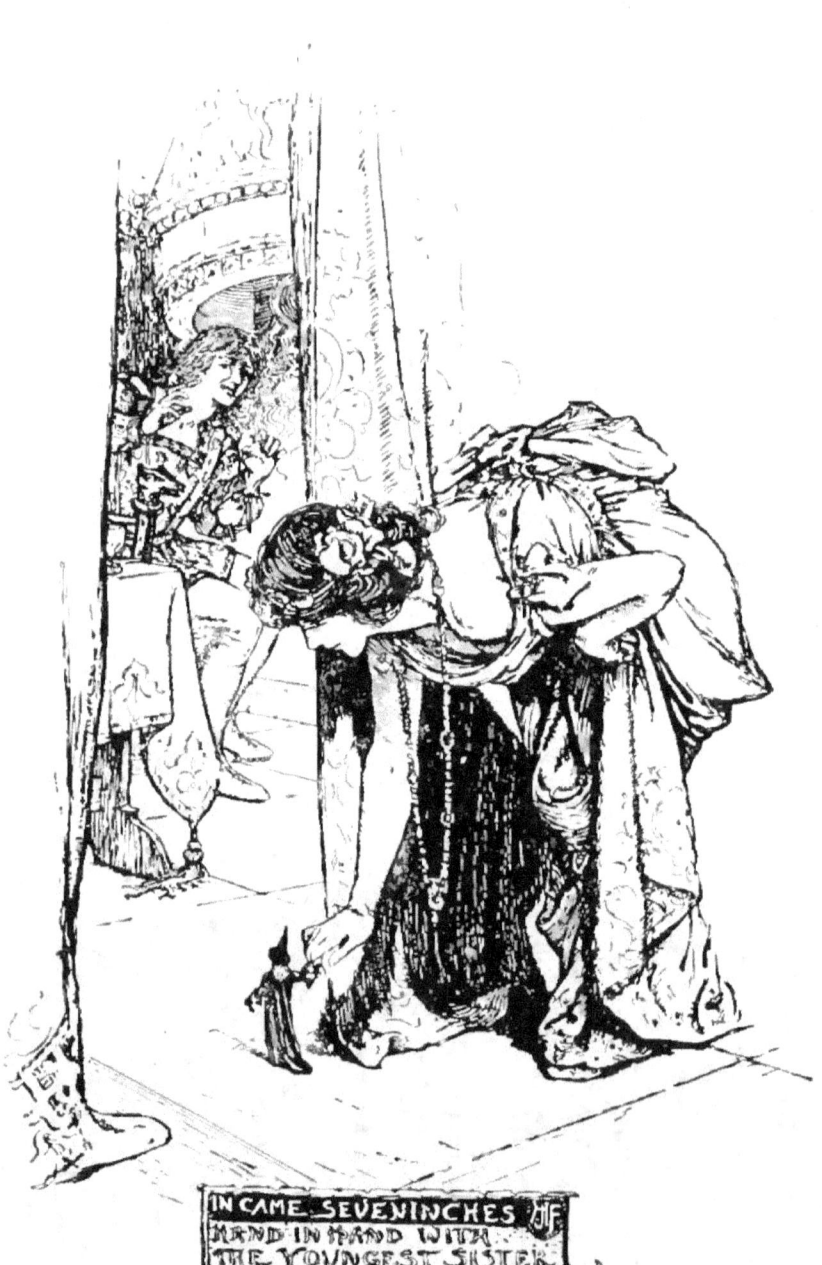

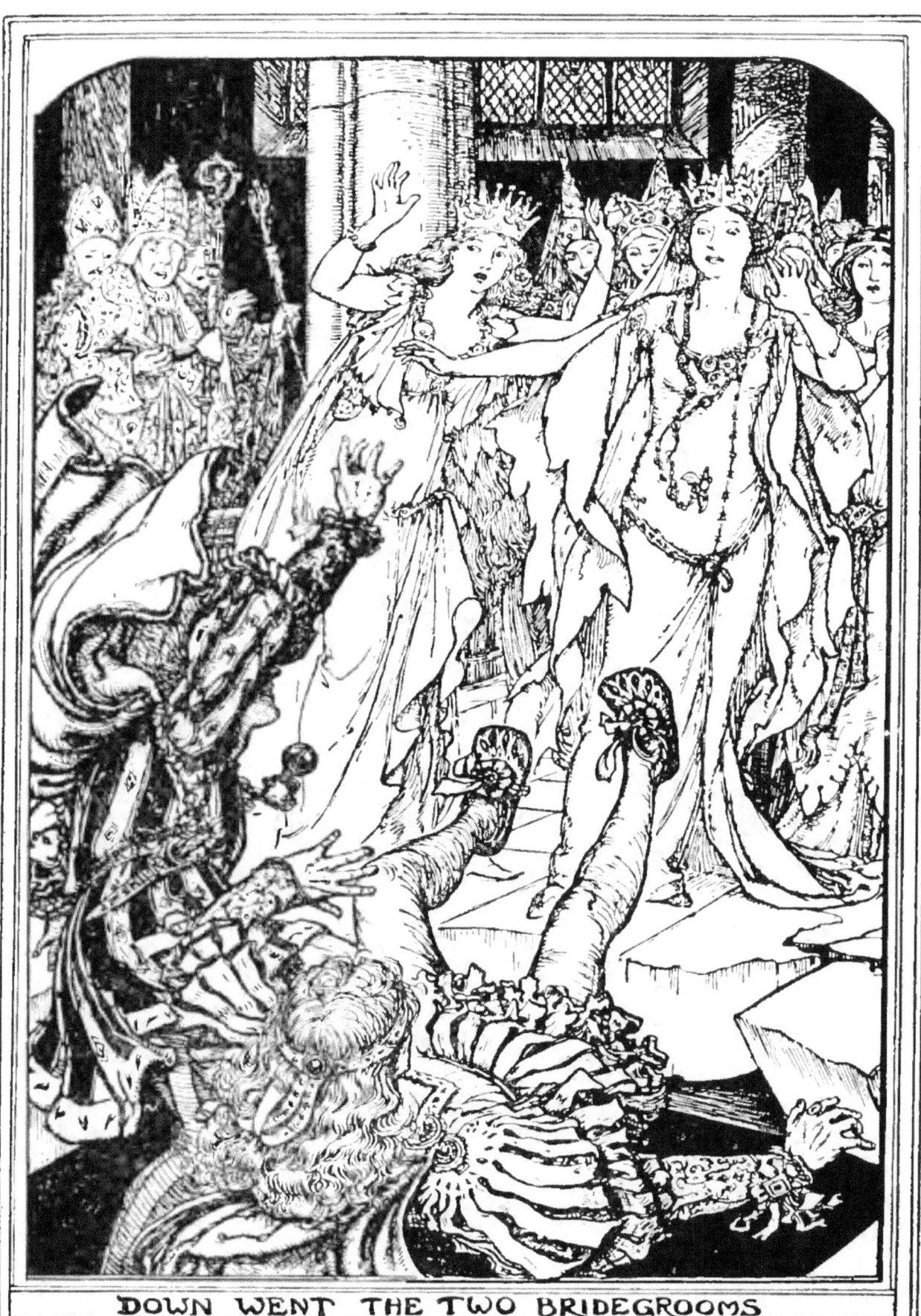

DOWN WENT THE TWO BRIDEGROOMS

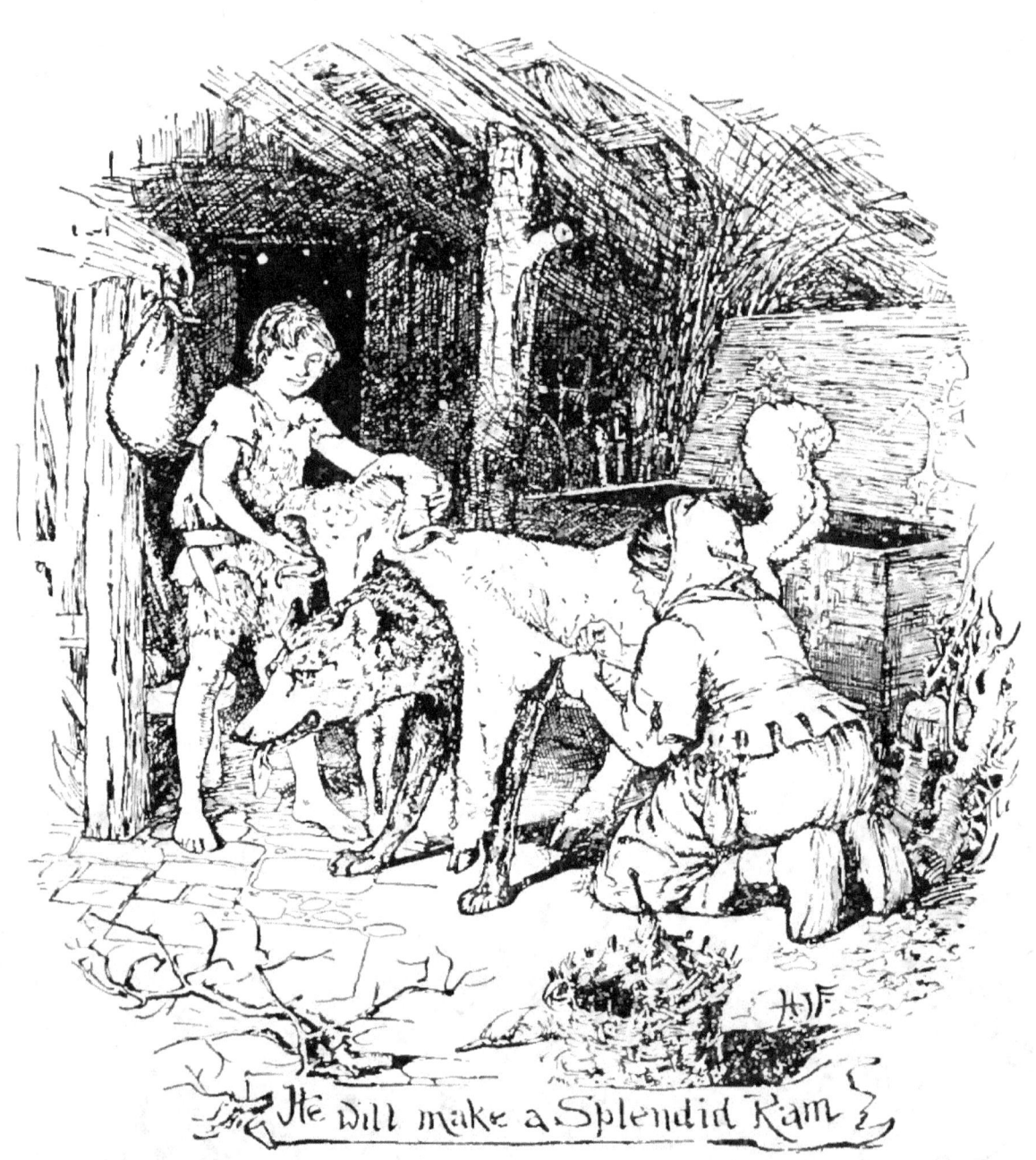

He will make a Splendid Ram

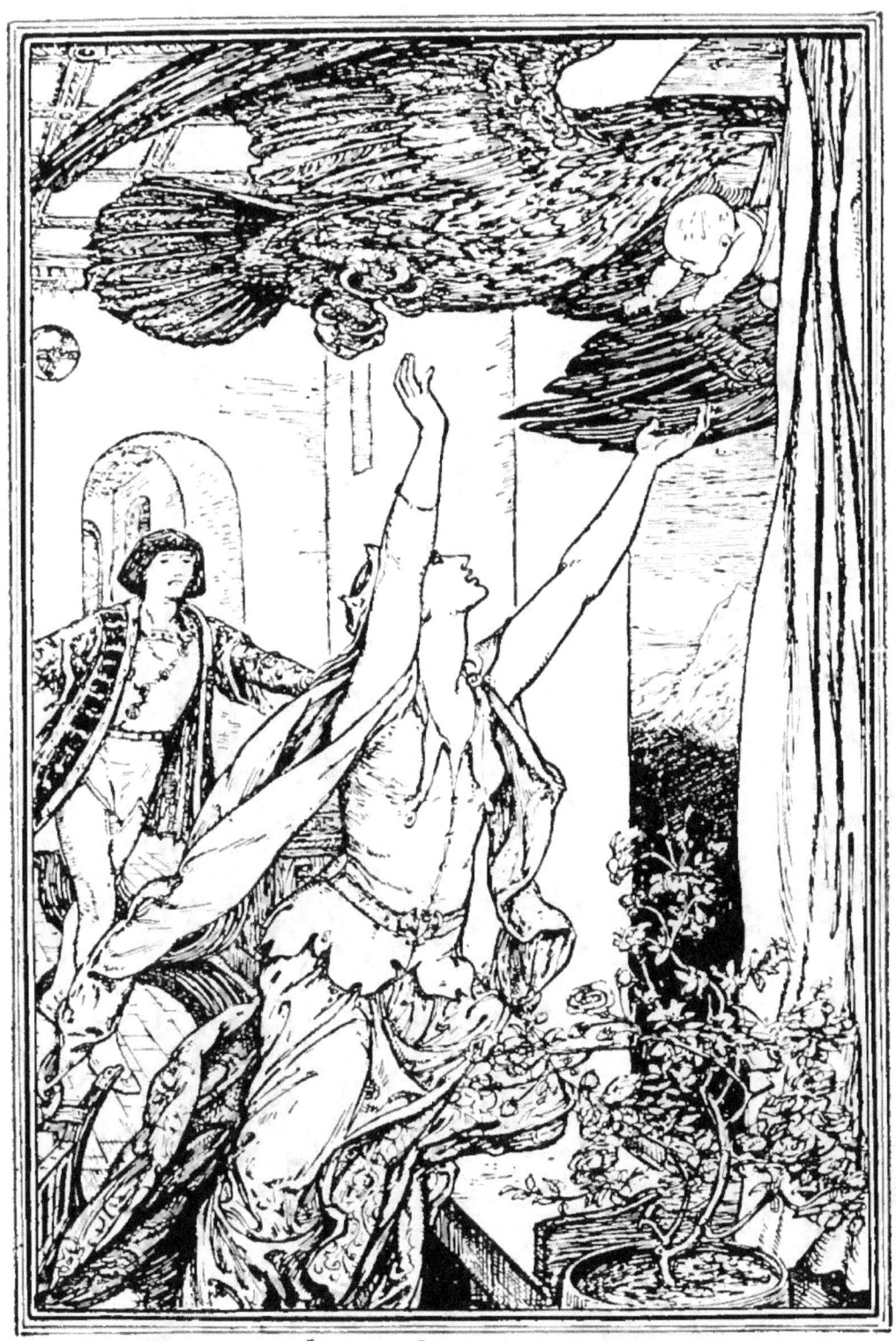

The Princess loses her first Baby.

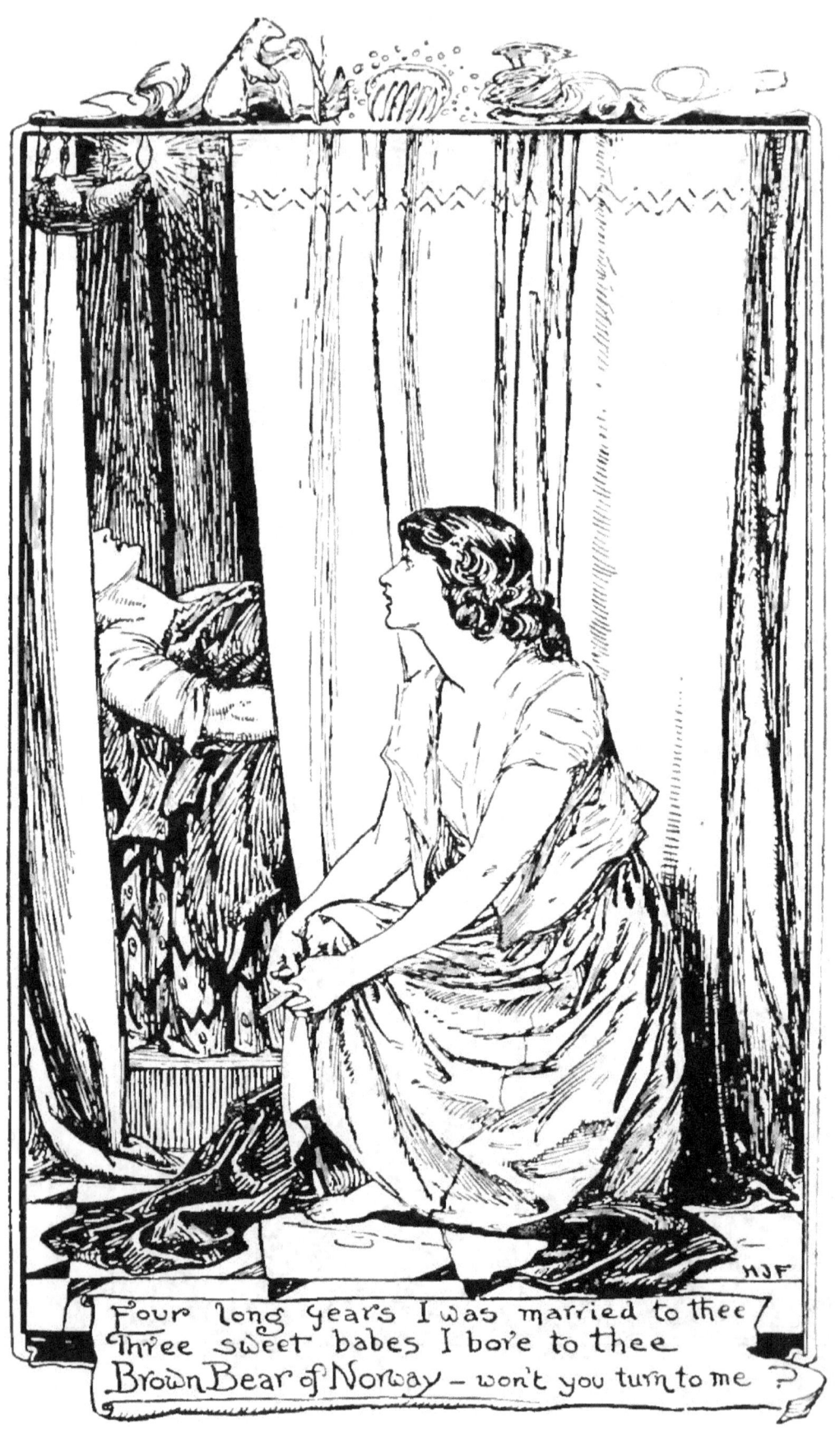

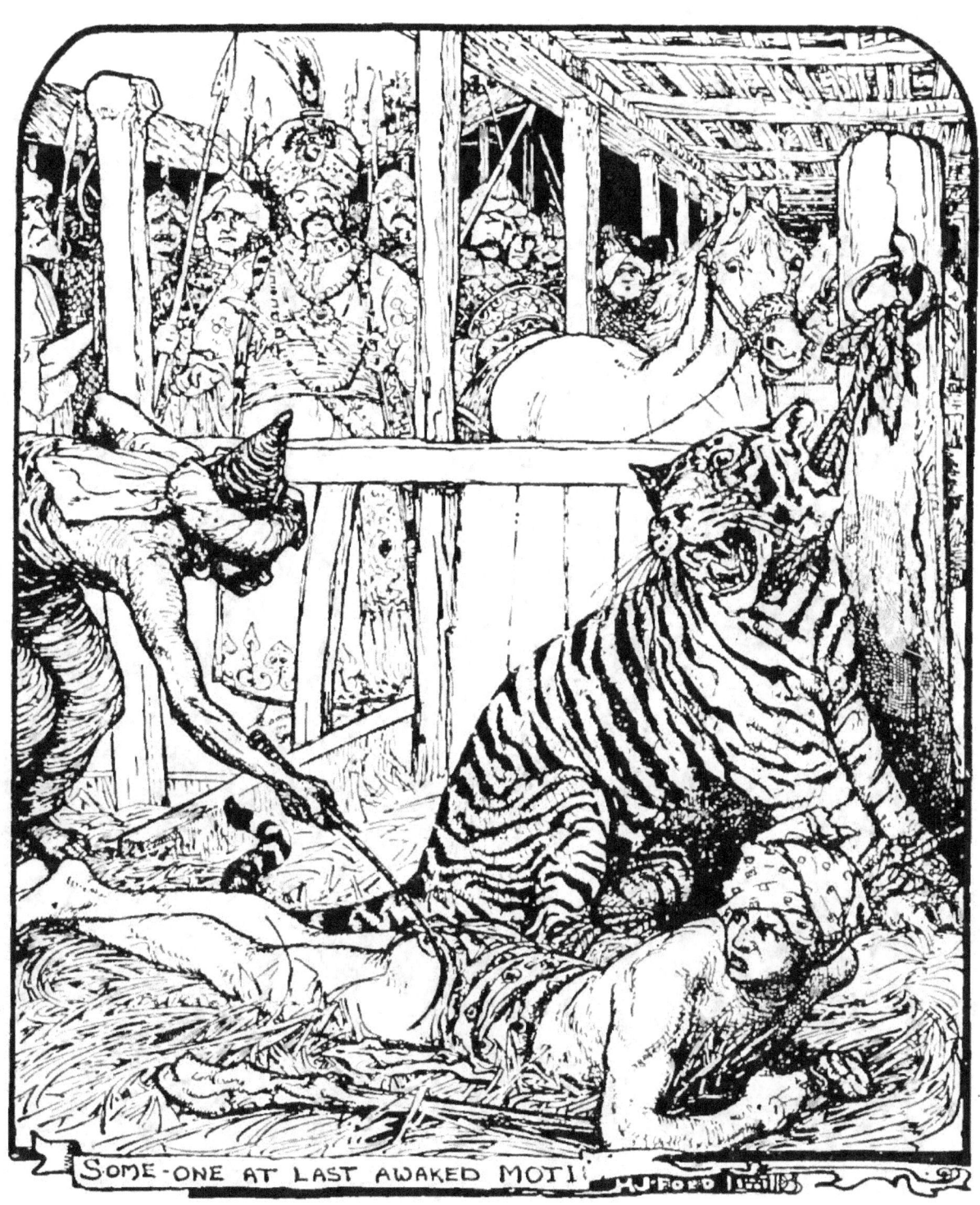
SOME-ONE AT LAST AWAKED MOTI

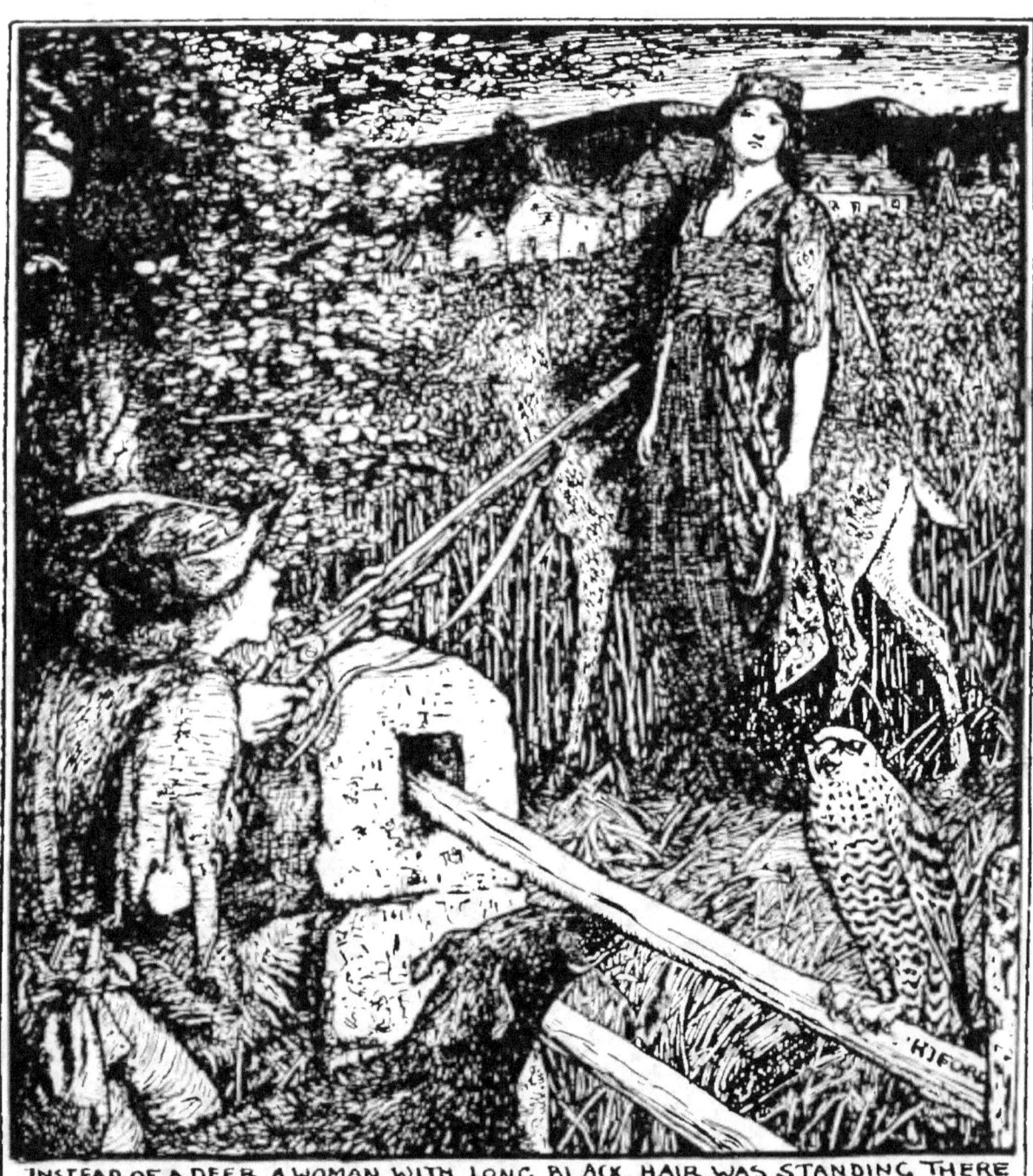
INSTEAD OF A DEER A WOMAN WITH LONG BLACK HAIR WAS STANDING THERE

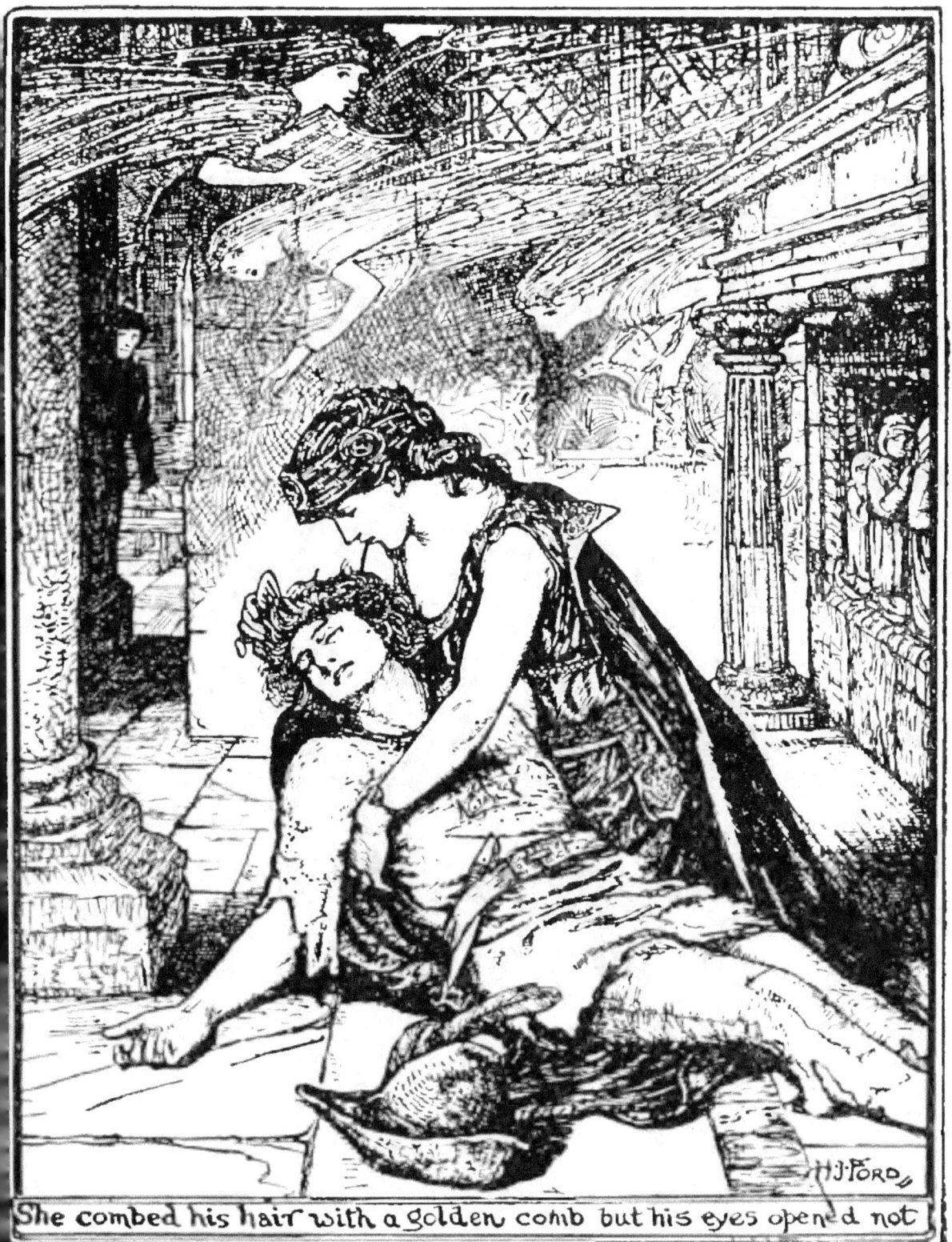
She combed his hair with a golden comb but his eyes opened not

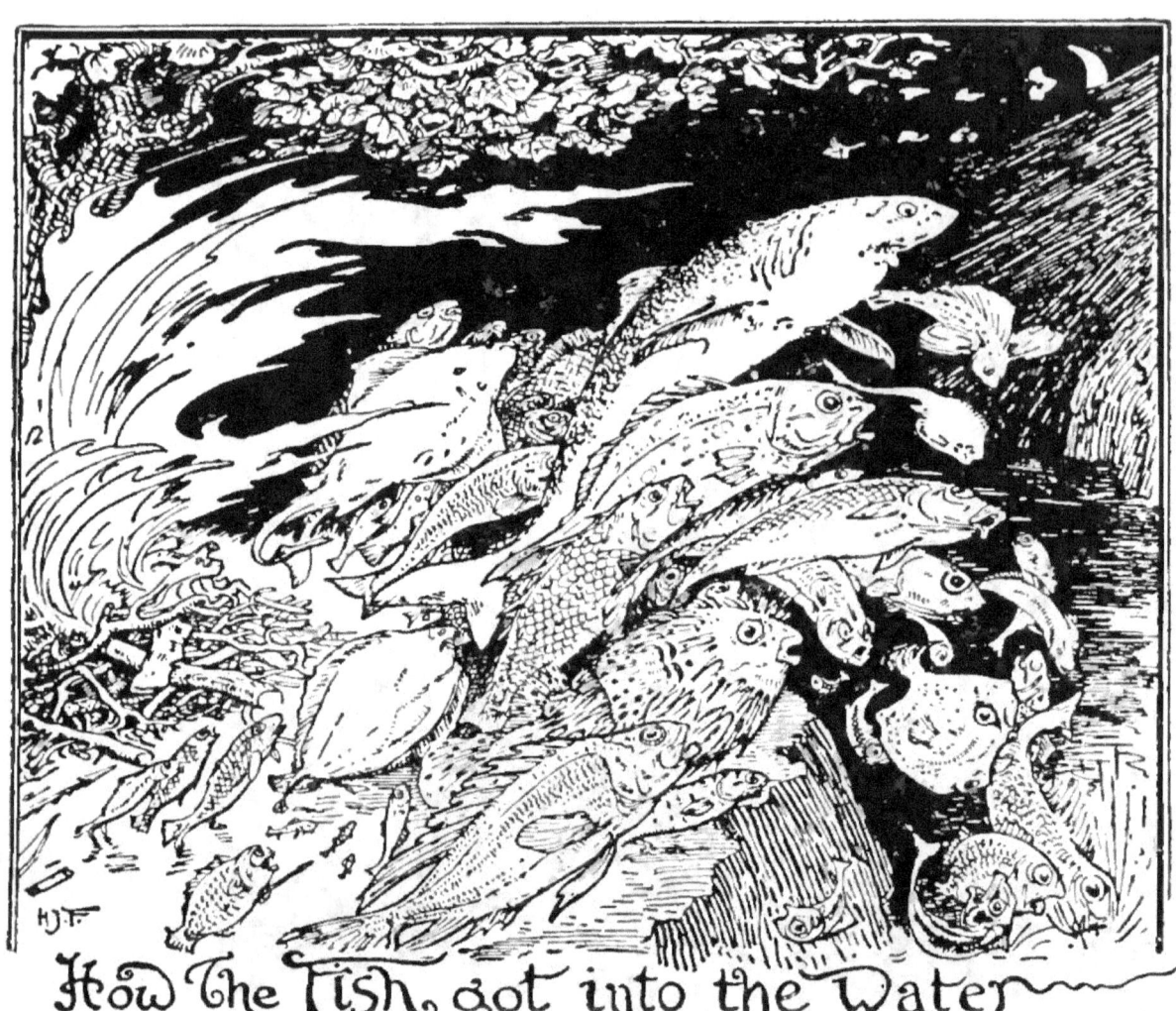
How the Fish got into the Water

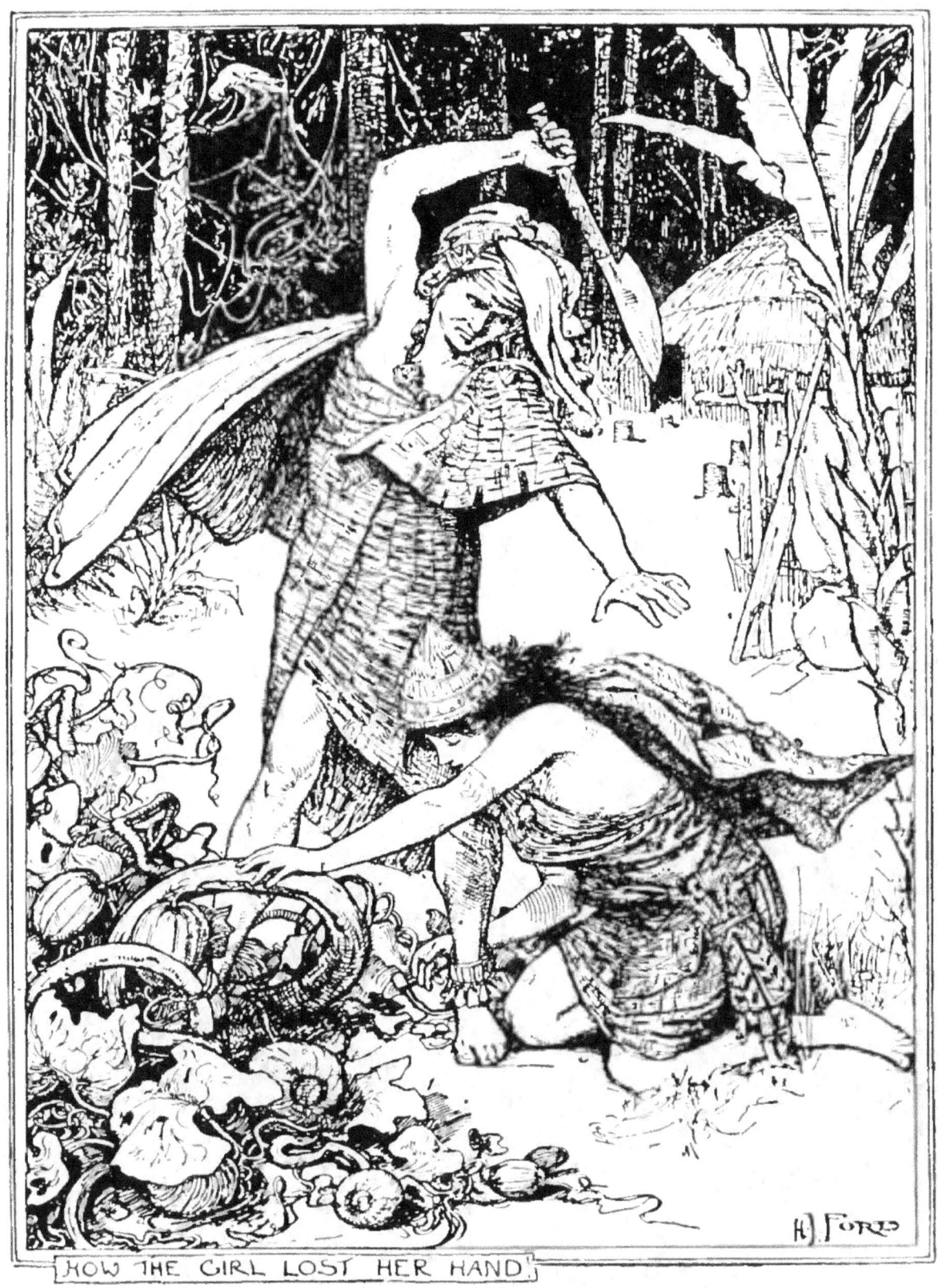
HOW THE GIRL LOST HER HAND

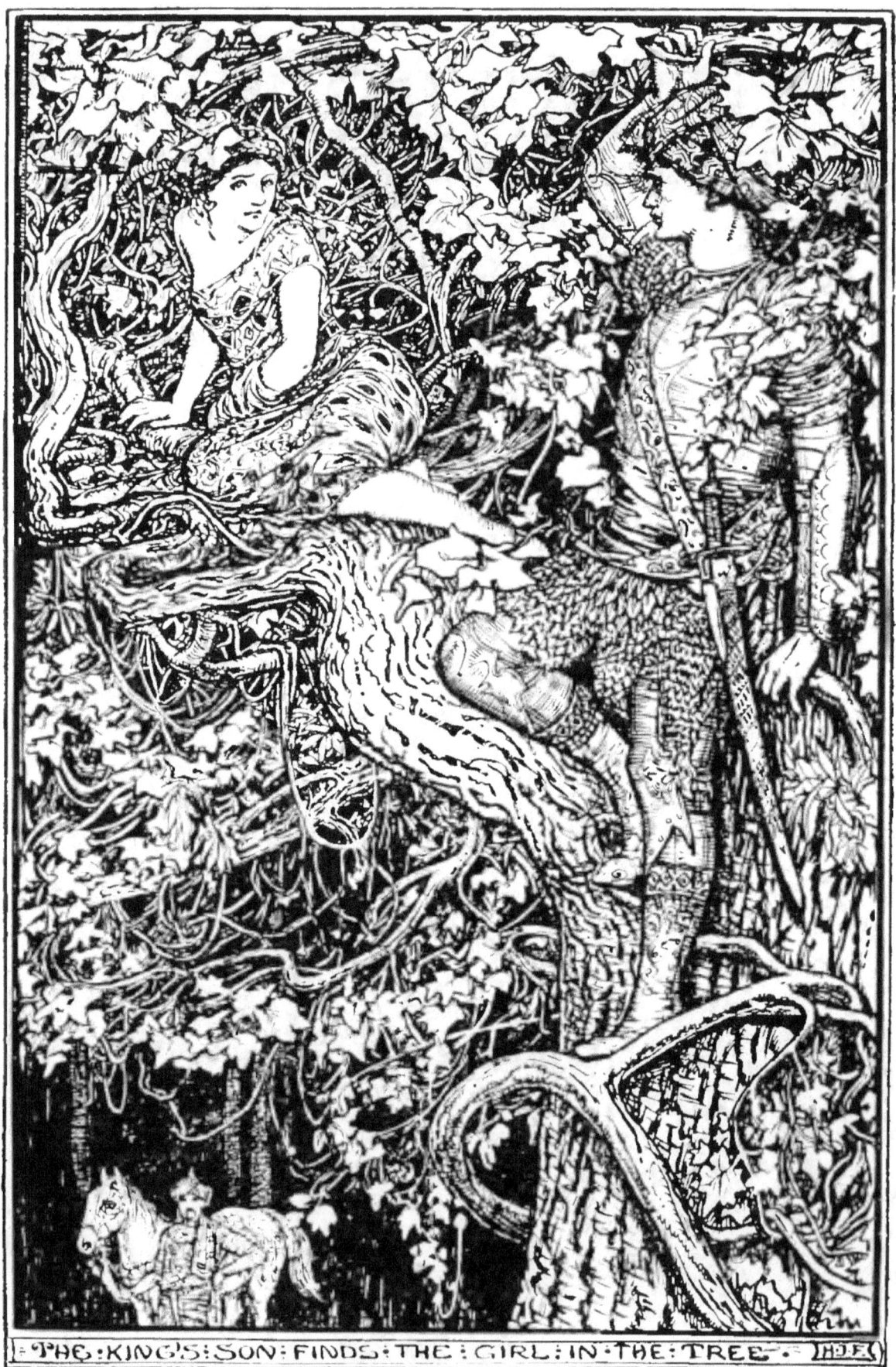
THE KING'S SON FINDS THE GIRL IN THE TREE

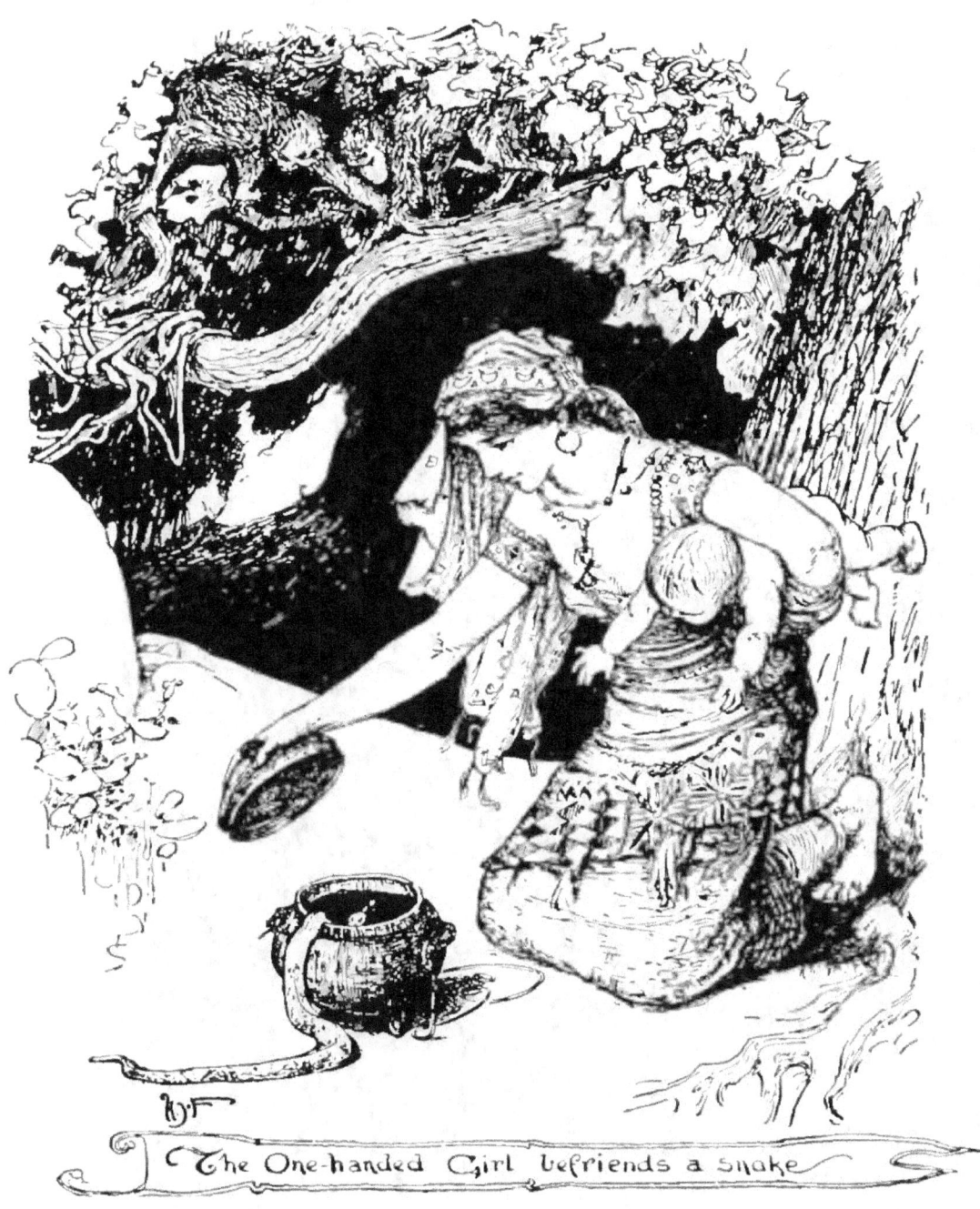

The One-handed Girl befriends a snake

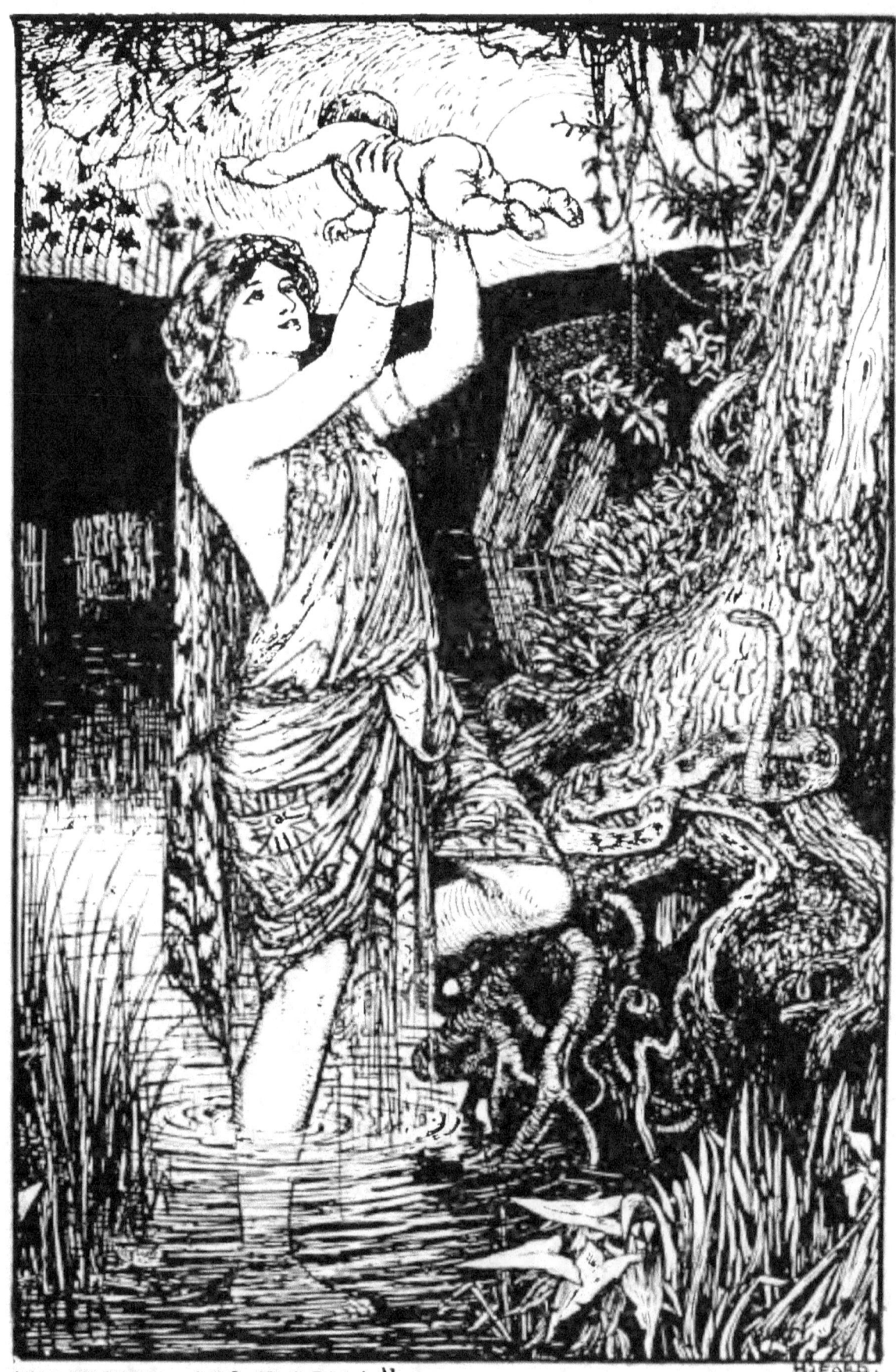

"MY BABY, MY BABY!"

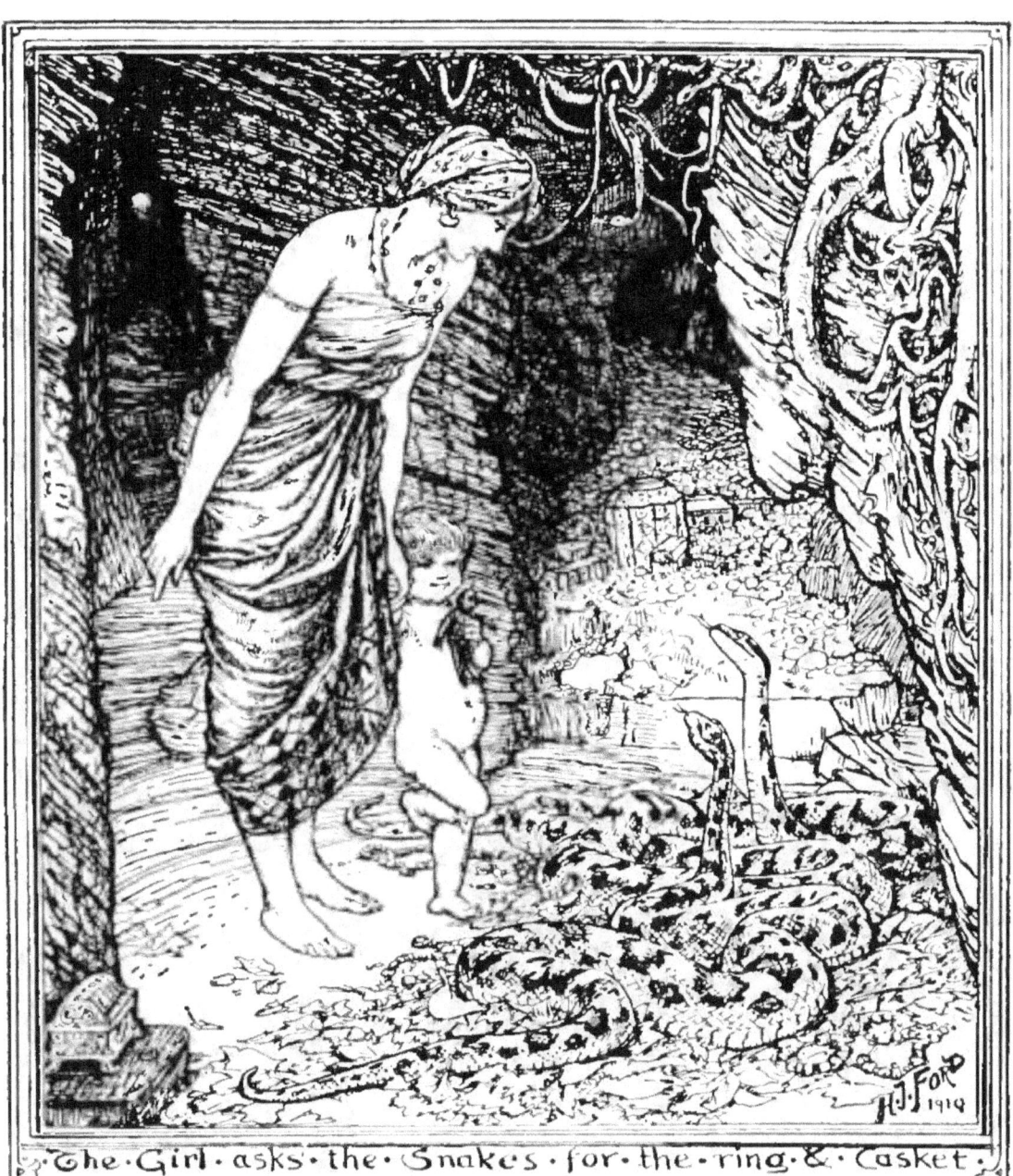
The Girl asks the Snakes for the ring & Casket

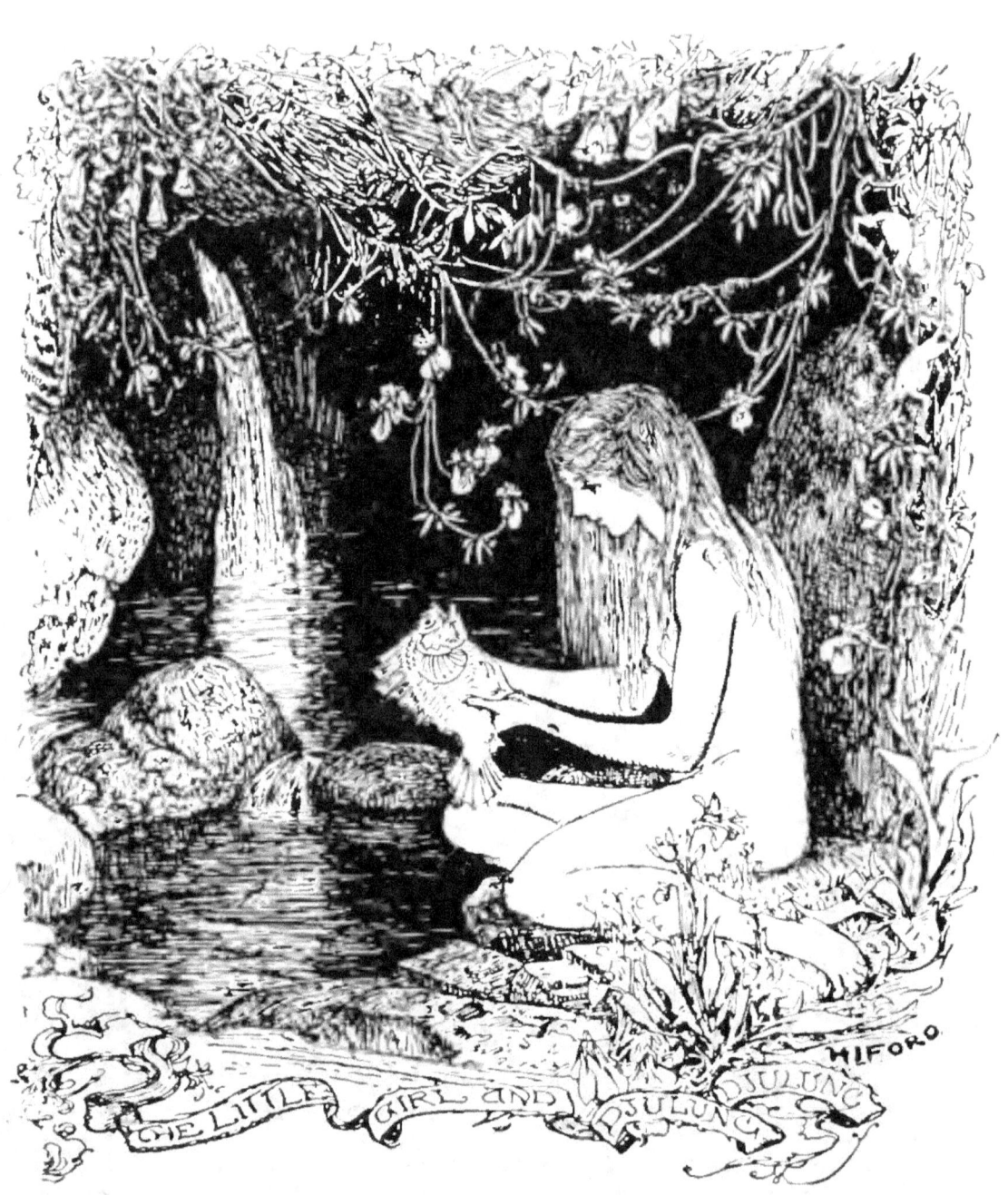
THE LITTLE GIRL AND DJULUNG

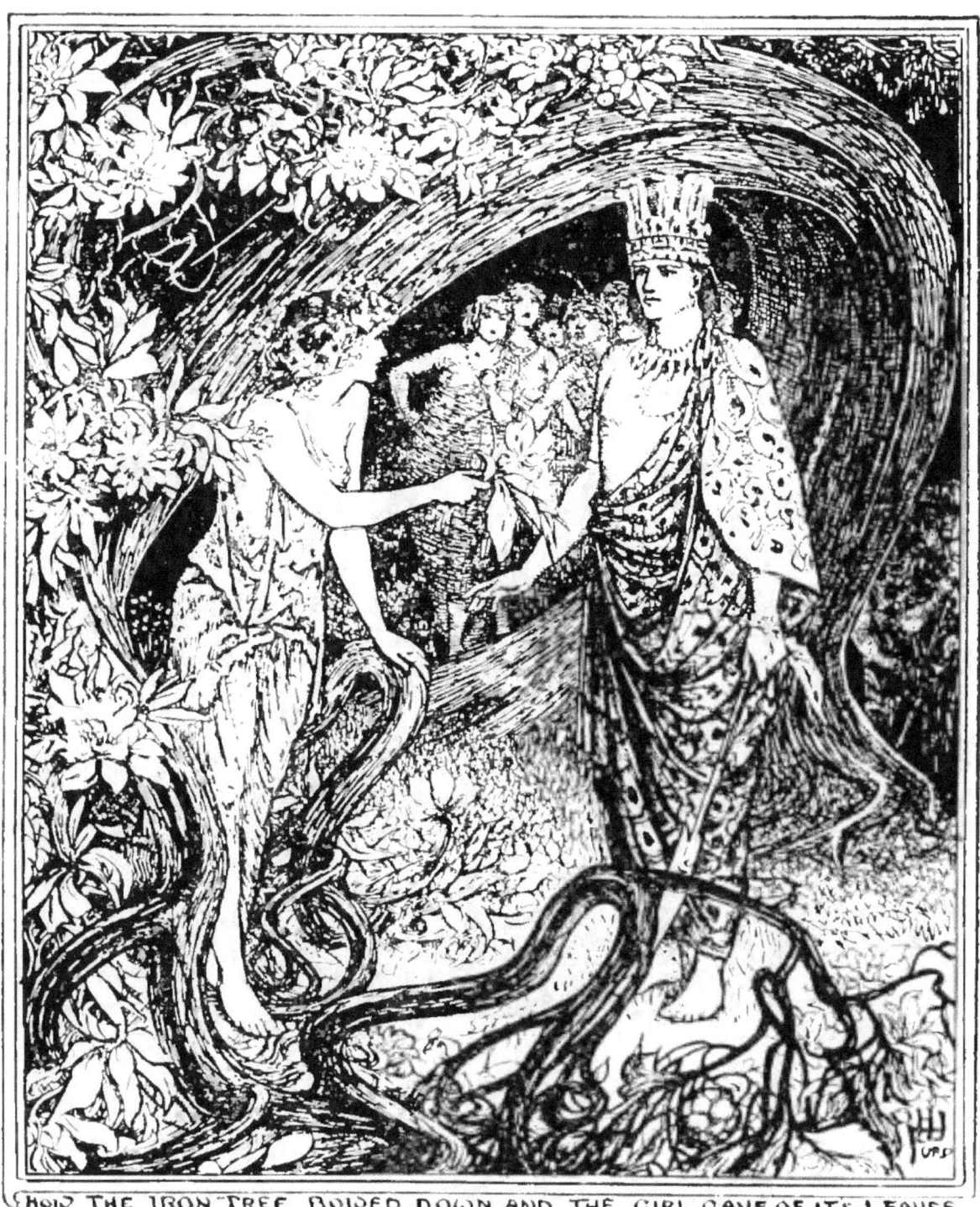

How the Iron-Tree bowed down and the girl gave of its leaves and flowers to the King.

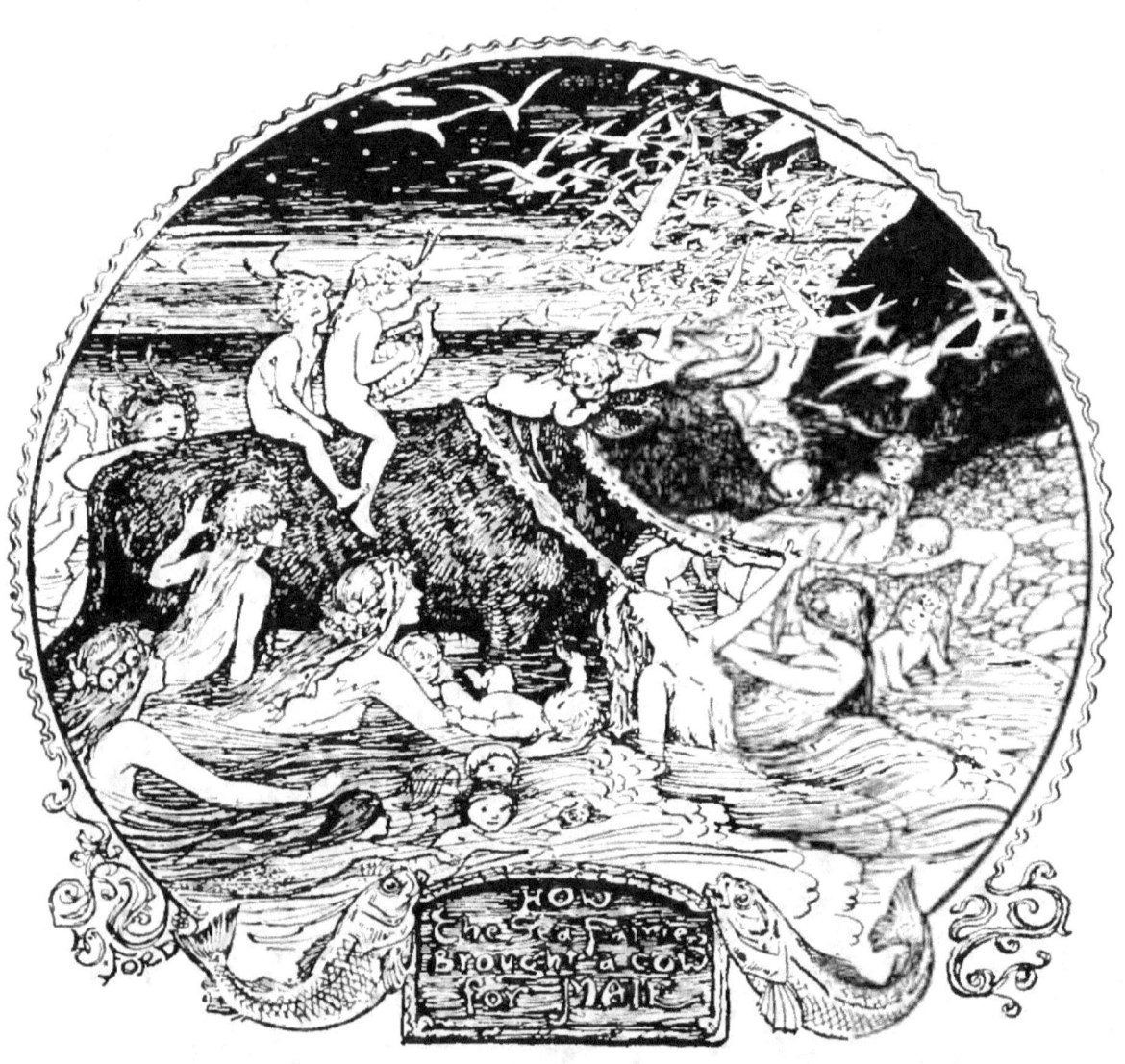

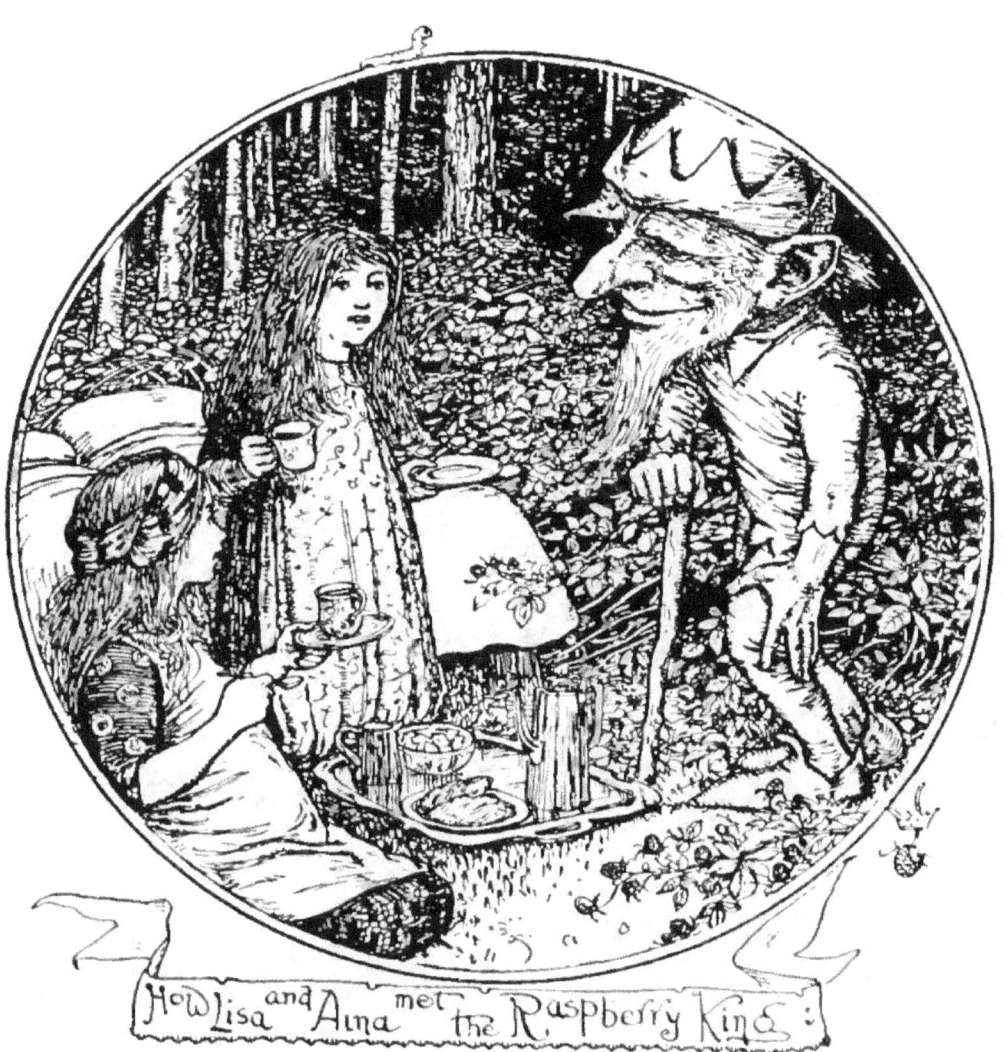
How Lisa and Aina met the Raspberry King

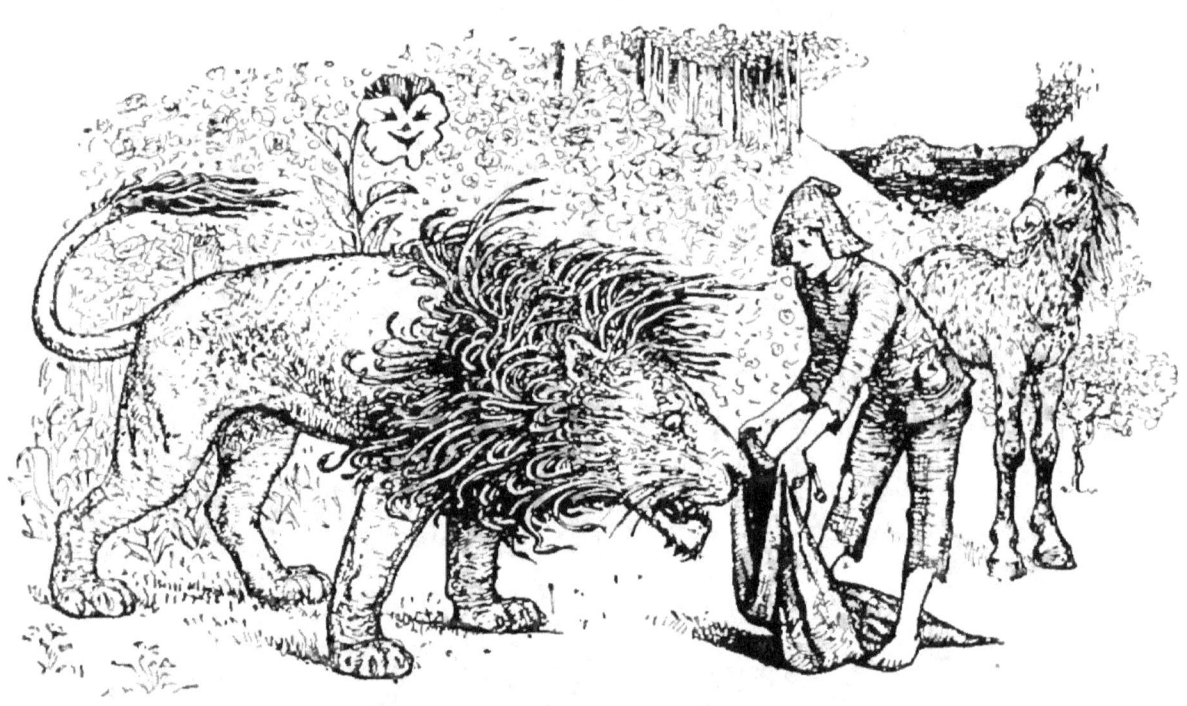

How Peronnik tricked the Viper-maned Lion with a bag

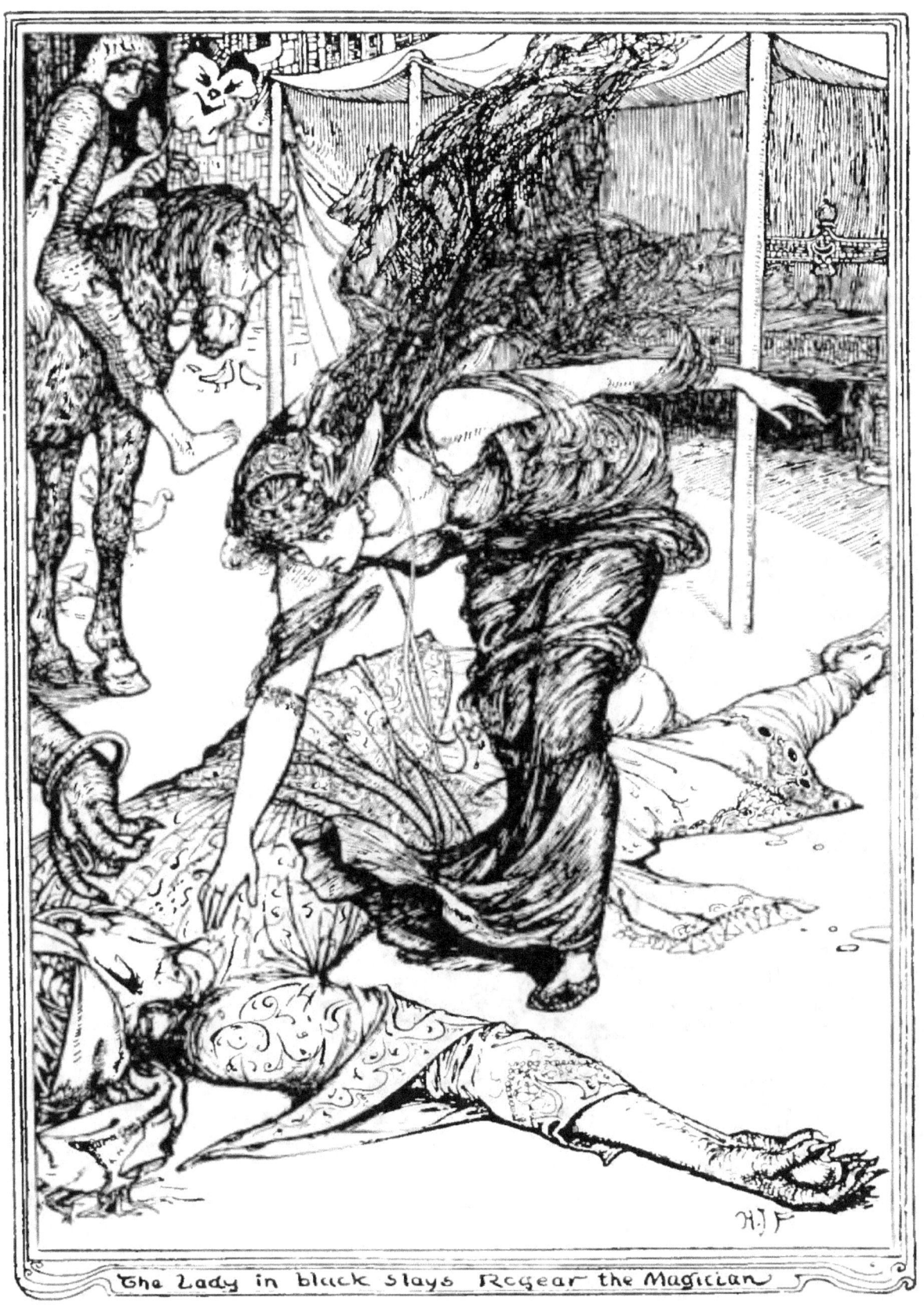
The Lady in black slays Regear the Magician

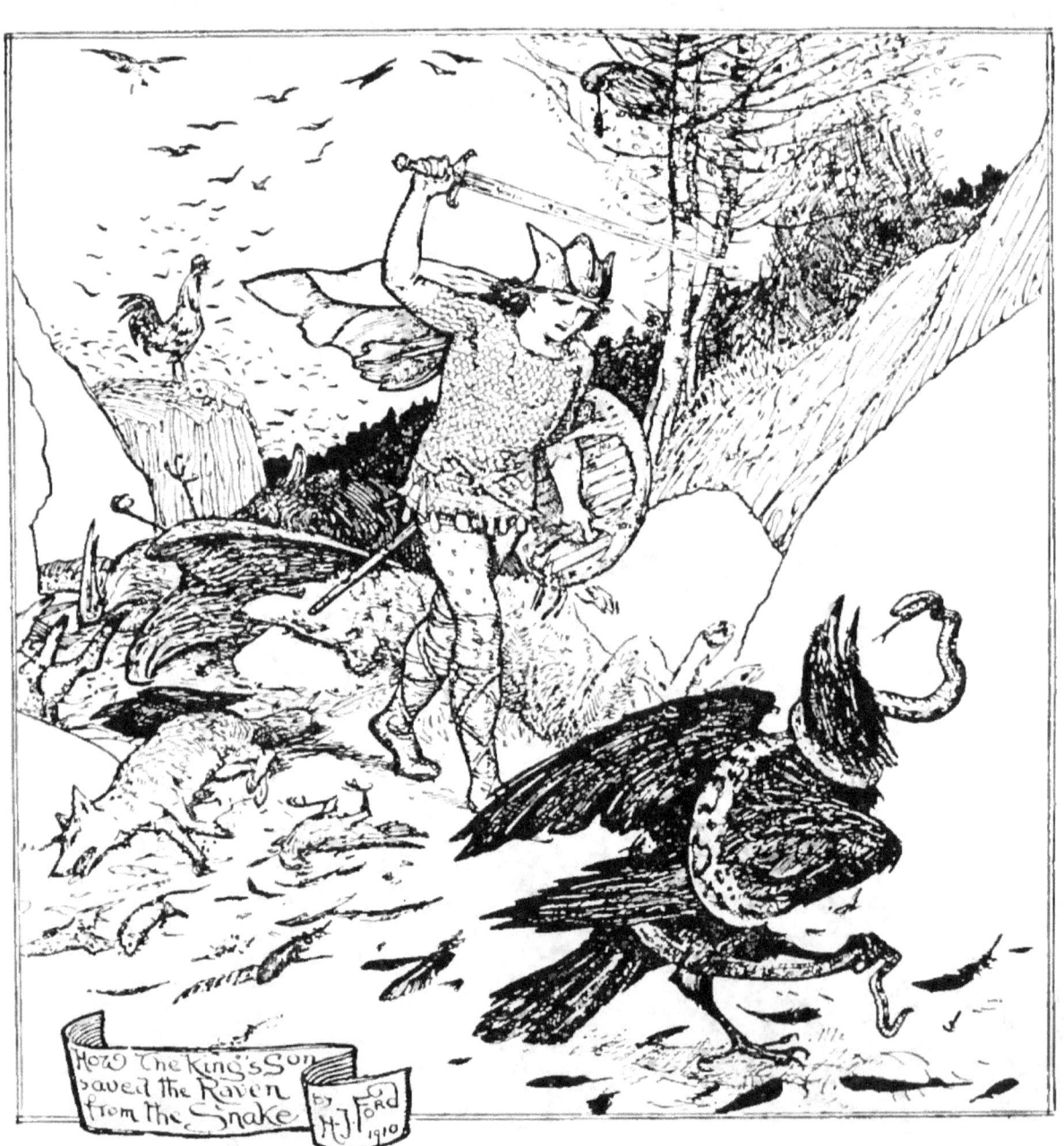
How the King's Son saved the Raven from the Snake

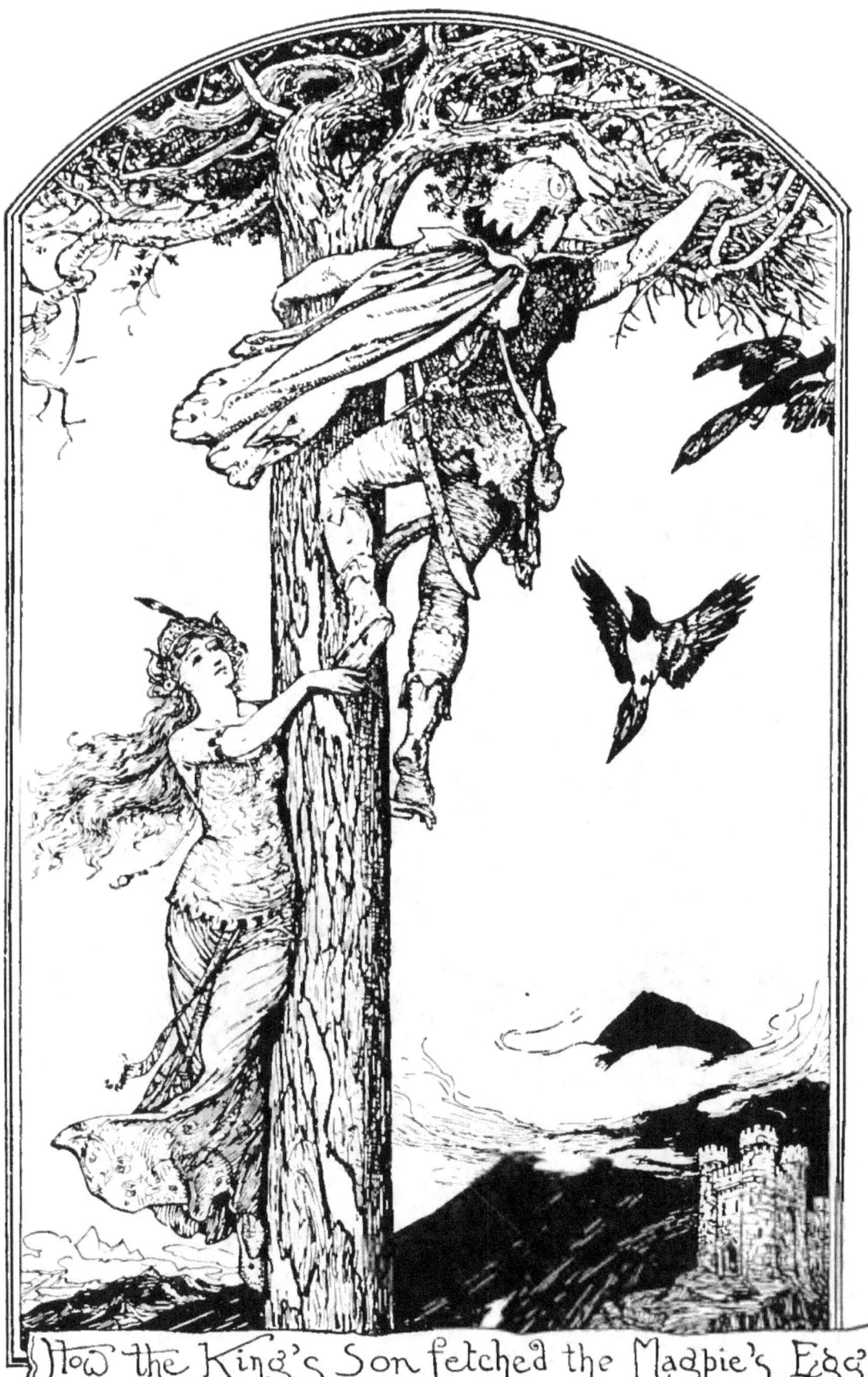
How the King's Son fetched the Magpie's Eggs

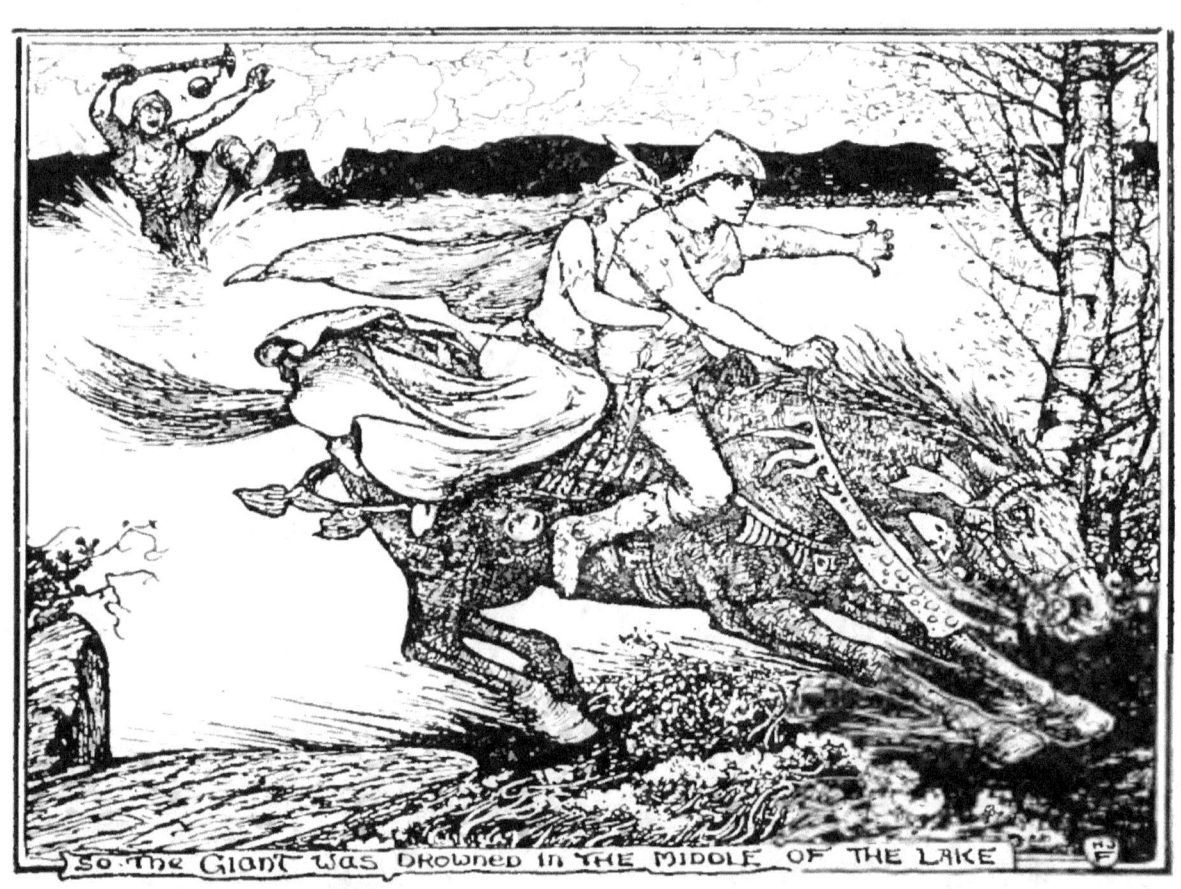
So the Giant was drowned in the middle of the lake

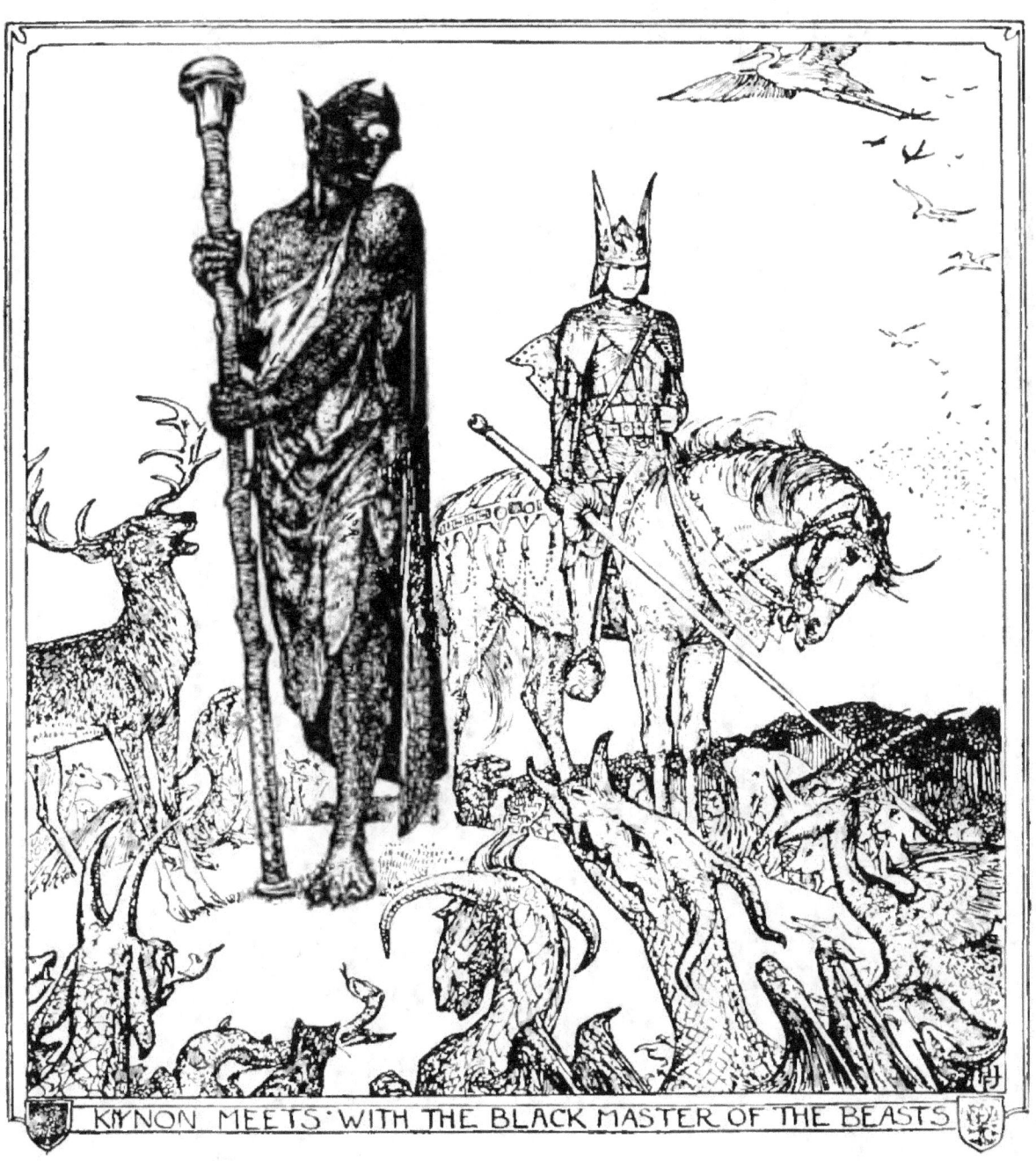
KYNON MEETS WITH THE BLACK MASTER OF THE BEASTS

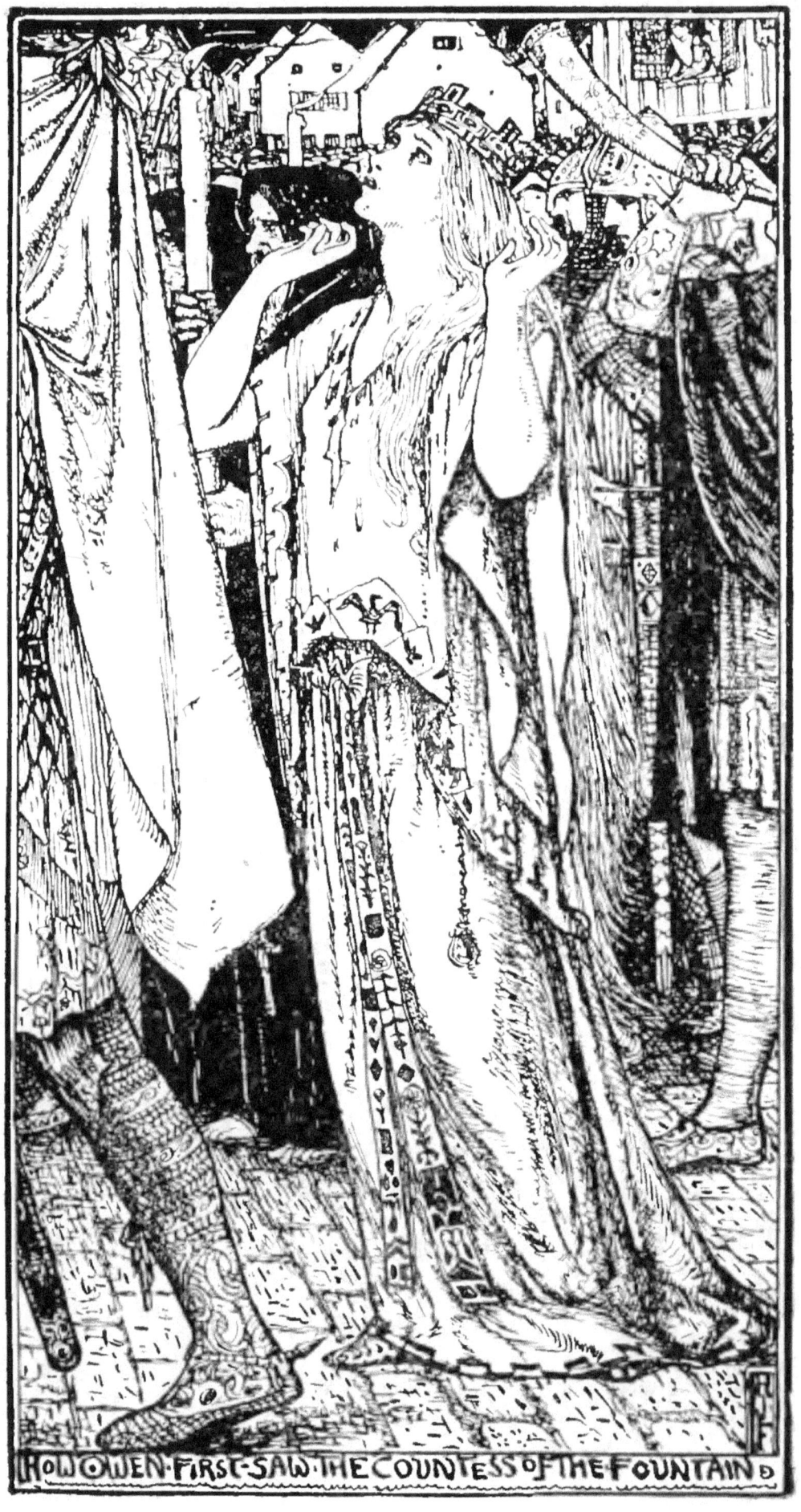

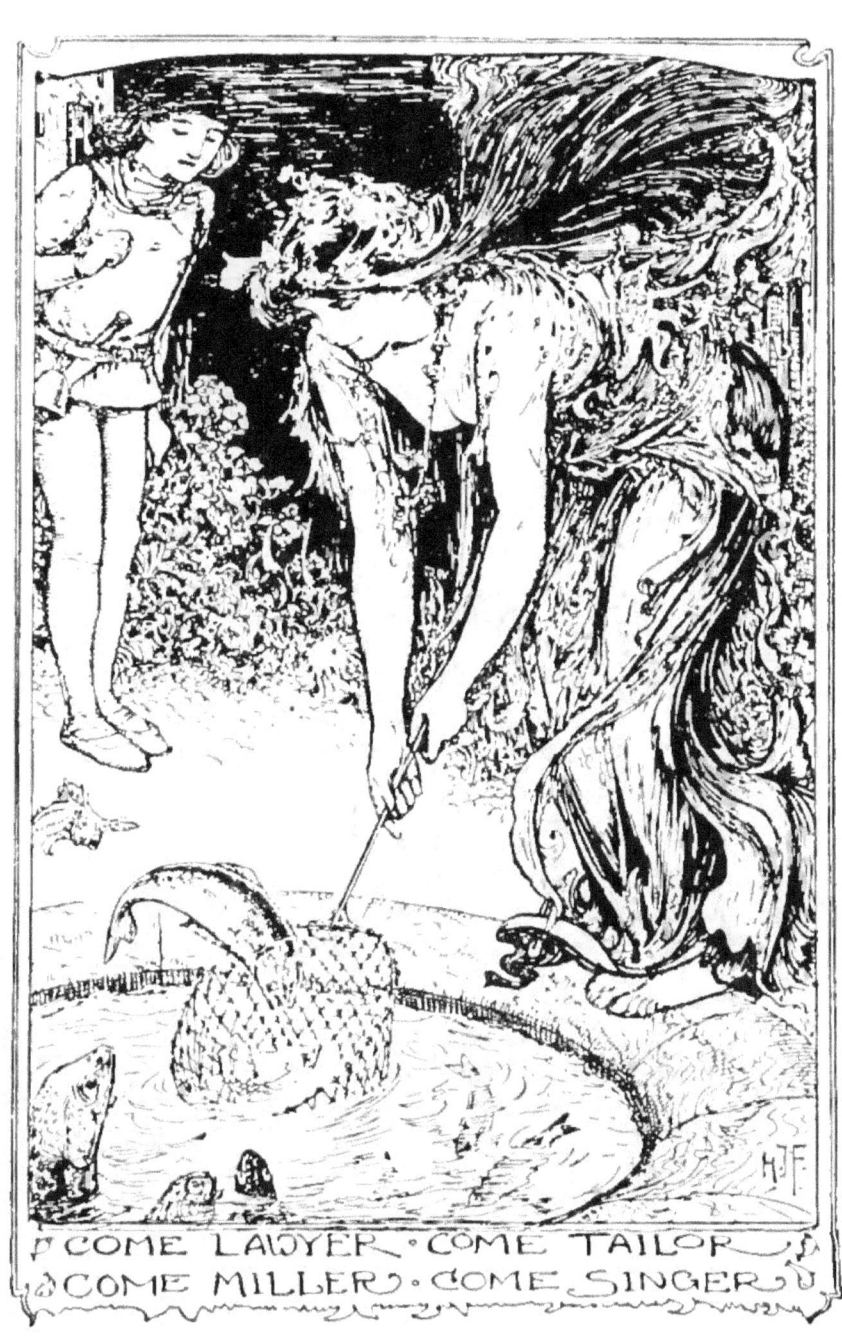

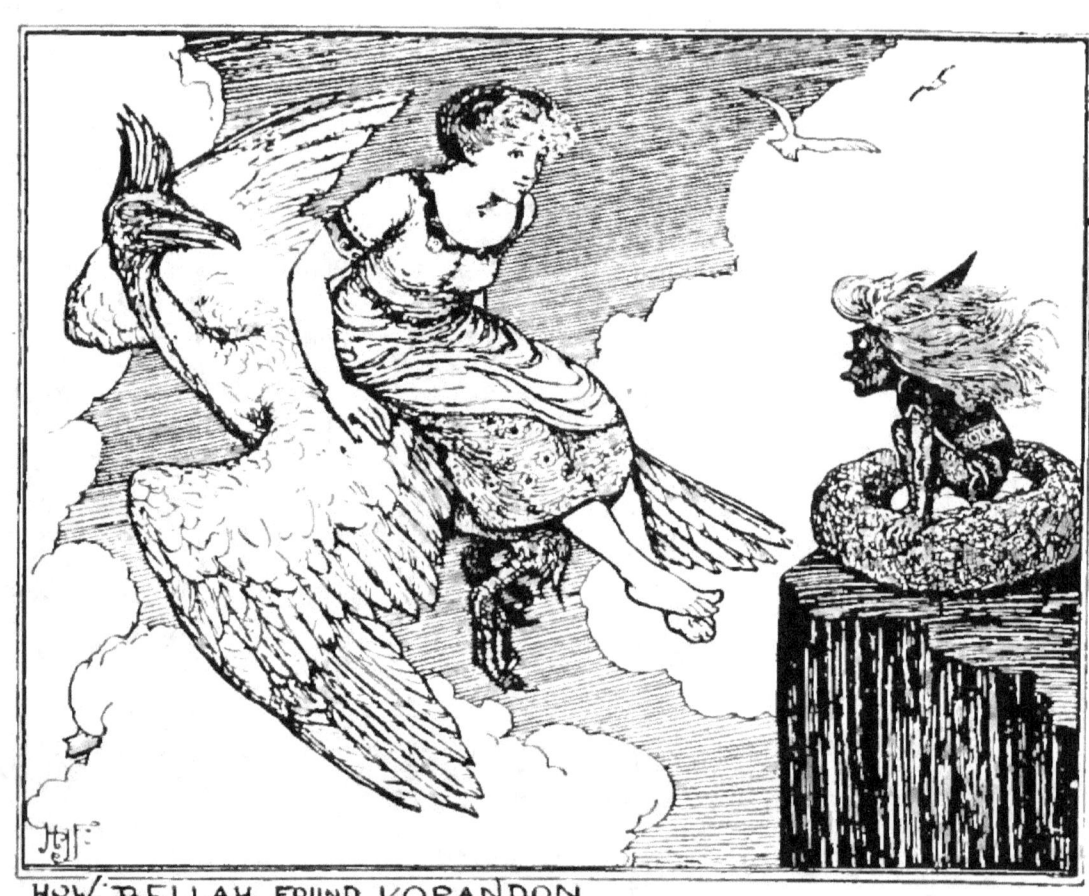
HOW BELLAH FOUND KORANDON

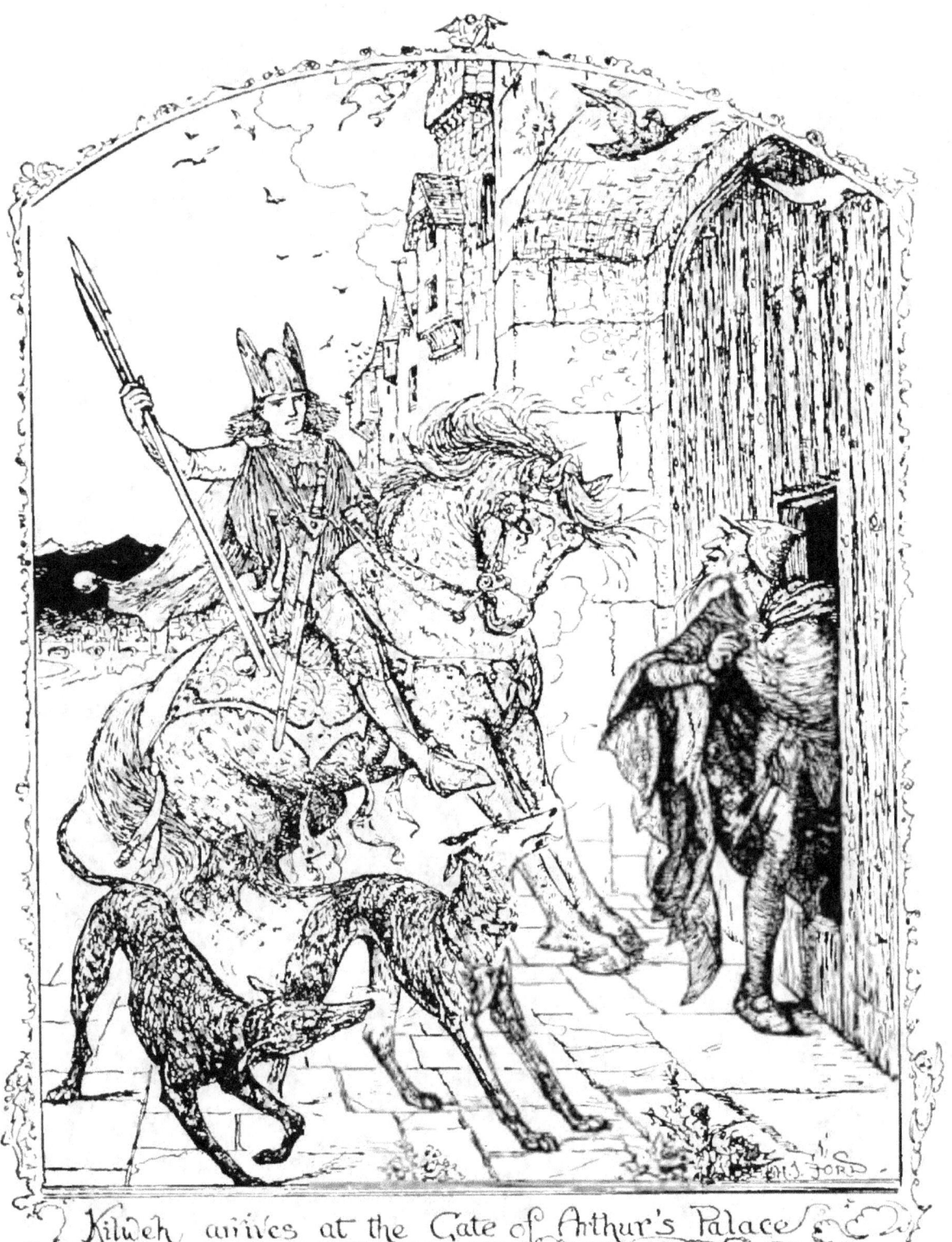

Kilweh arrives at the Gate of Arthur's Palace

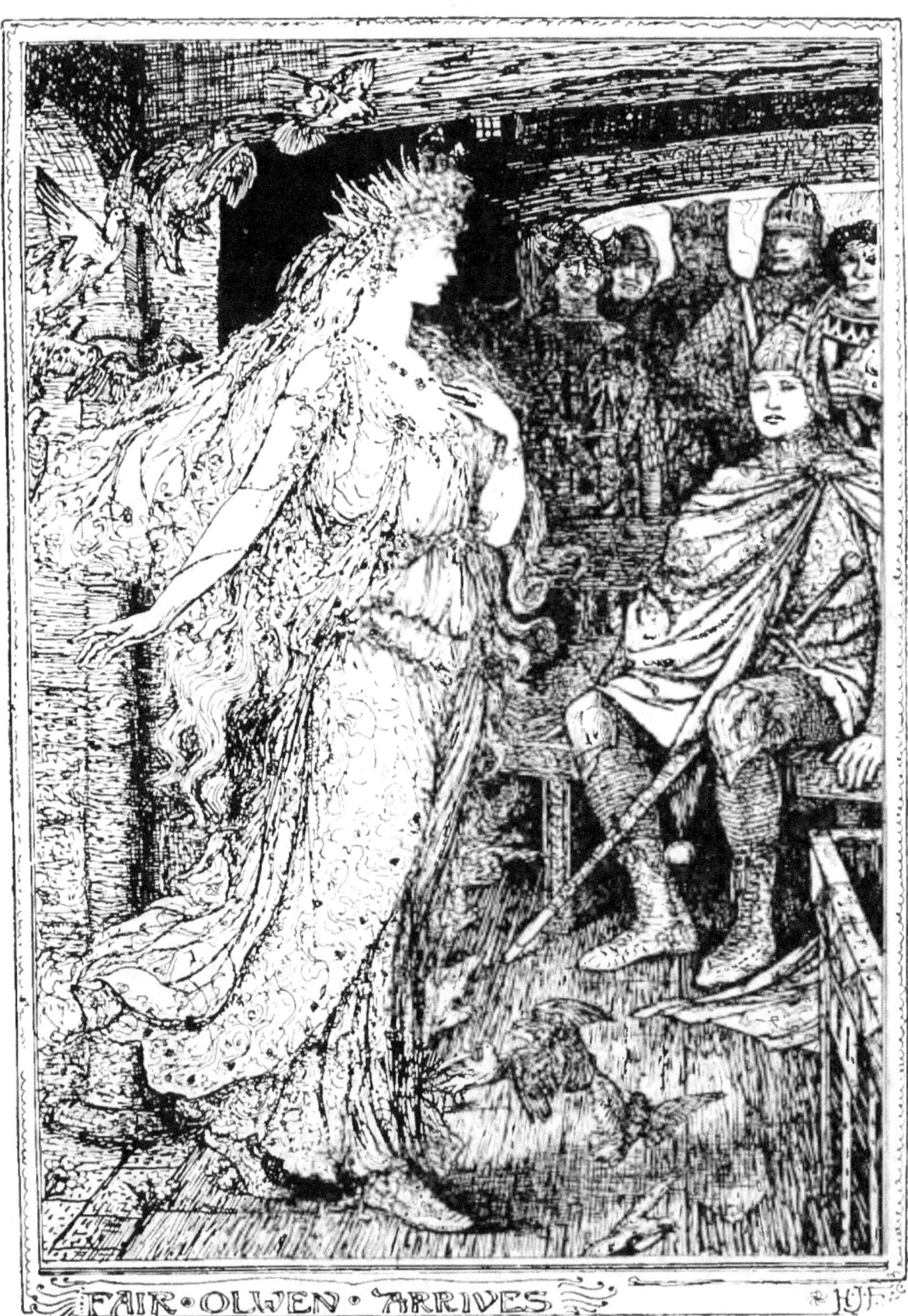
FAIR OLWEN ARRIVES

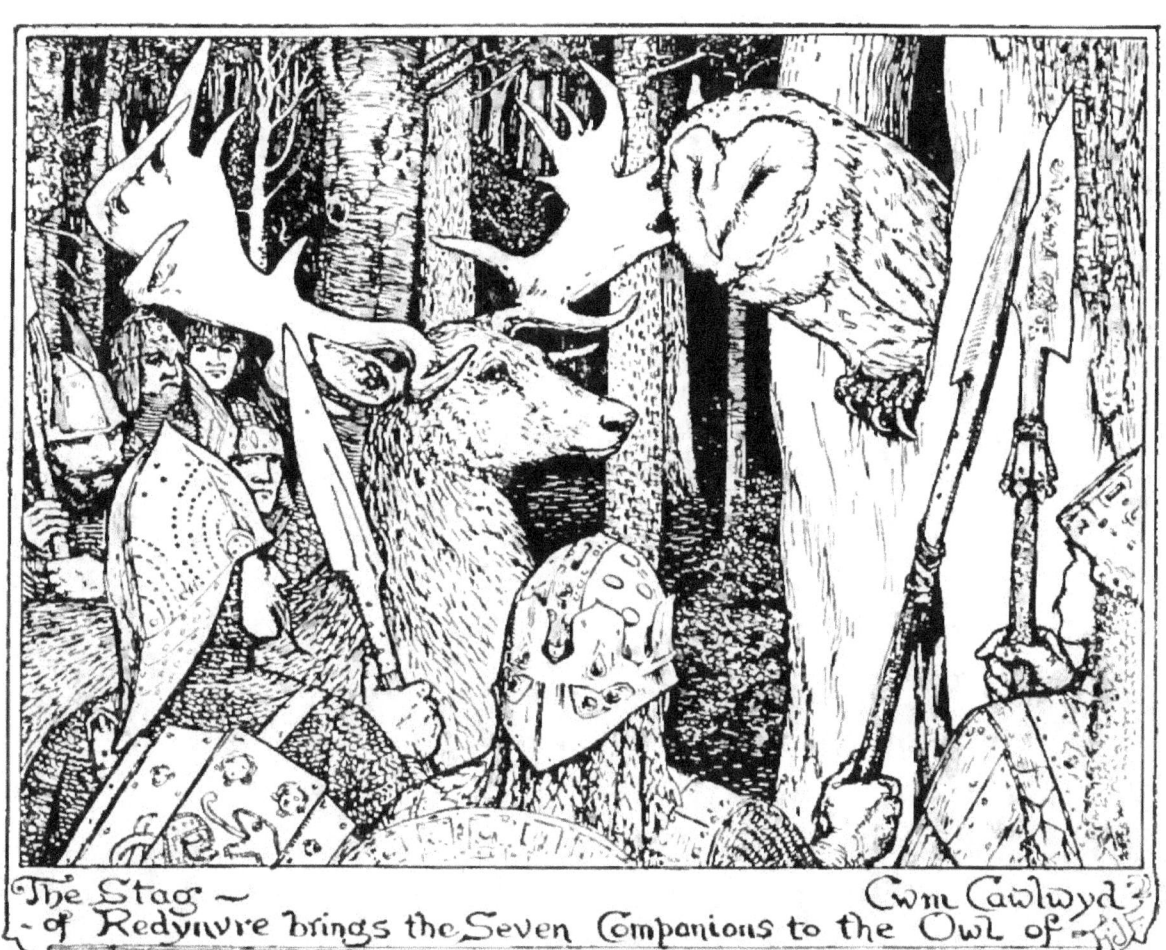
The Stag of Redynvre brings the Seven Companions to the Owl of Cwm Cawlwyd

www.ingramcontent.com/pod-product-compliance
Lightning Source LLC
Chambersburg PA
CBHW082222220526
45470CB00010B/3268